W9-BKA-149

MAR 8 1995	DATE DUE	
MAR 0 6 1996		
JUN 3 0 1998		
FEB 1 5 2005		

Putting on Appearances
Gender and Advertising

IN THE SERIES

Women in the Political Economy,
edited by Ronnie J. Steinberg

Putting on
Appearances

Gender and Advertising

Diane Barthel

TEMPLE UNIVERSITY PRESS
Philadelphia

Temple University Press, Philadelphia 19122
Copyright © 1988 by Temple University. All rights reserved
Published 1988
Printed in the United States of America

The paper used in this publication meets the minimum
requirements of American National Standard for Information
Sciences—Permanence of Paper for Printed Library Materials,
ANSI Z39.48-1984

Library of Congress Cataloging-in-Publication Data
Barthel, Diane L., 1949–
Putting on appearances : gender and advertising / Diane Barthel.
     p. cm.—(Women in the political economy)
Includes index.
ISBN 0-87722-528-1 (alk. paper)
1. Sex role in advertising—United States. 2. Visual
communication—United States—Psychological aspects. 3. Imagery
(Psychology) I. Title. II. Series.
HF5827.B37 1988
659.1′042—dc19

                                                            87-20010
                                                                 CIP

To David

Contents

Acknowledgments

Various colleagues, students, and friends offered encouragement during the researching and writing of this book. I would like to take this opportunity to thank Barbara Bader, David Bouchier, Rose Laub Coser, Kenneth Feldman, Jenean Marchese, Michael Schwartz, Judith Tanur, members of the Feminist Seminar, and students in my Women and Men courses. I appreciate their interest and support in this effort to get beyond appearances.

Putting on Appearances
Gender and Advertising

ONE

Introduction

Be the first to wear Poison
The Fragrance Sensation from
Europe

KL Homme "For the man who
lives on the edge"

New Wide Solid Secret—
Strong enough for a man,
but with curved comfort for a
woman.

Advertising is about appearances. It is also about information, but what interests us, what excites us in and about advertising is how objects, or products, become ideas, how they become gifted with appearances: how they make appearances and help *us* make appearances. This does not happen through magic. It happens through the advertiser's skill at positioning the product, creating an image, "finding a place for it to live in our minds."[1] Information becomes part of appearance. When Joy perfume advertised that it was the costliest perfume in the world, that was information of a sort. But it also created an appearance.

The object gains an appearance whose own magic and content it promises to pour onto its consumers. Advertising is not just about the object's appearance but about personal appearances: how we look to others, how we think of ourselves. Advertisers know that the critical issue is "what will it do for *me*?" We seldom tire of ourselves, not when we can find constant renewal through the purchase of new products. Advertising, then, is about creating a relationship between subjects

1

and objects. The identity, the appearance, of each is critical, as are the economic, social, and cultural ties that bind object to subject.

Karl Marx spoke of the process whereby objects gain identities. For him, the critical moment came when the object appeared separate and separated from the conditions of its own production, when workers no longer recognized and claimed it as their own handiwork. The worker became alienated from his or her product. Thus liberated, the product assumed a power that Marx likened to the power granted religious fetish objects: "In order, therefore, to find an analogy we must take flight into the misty realm of religion. There the products of the human brain appear as autonomous figures endowed with a life of their own, which enter into relations both with each other and with the human race. So it is," wrote Marx, "in the world of commodities with the products of men's hands. I call this the fetishism which attaches itself to the products of labor as soon as they are produced as commodities, and is therefore insepara-ble from the production of commodities."[2]

A different viewpoint is provided by Georg Simmel. Simmel believed that we value goods in order not to worship them or surrender power to them. Rather, we express our identity in and through goods; they represent one important cultural mode for the articulation of the self. "Ownership is not, as it superficially appears to be, a passive acceptance of objects, but an acting with and upon them. Ownership, however comprehen-sive and unlimited, can do with things nothing other than provide an opportunity for the will of the Ego to find expression in them. For to own something actually means that the object does not resist my intentions, that they can prevail over it."[3] Money provides more than power over goods or products; it also gives us power over people. We need not enter into social relation-ships when we can simply buy human services.

Simmel himself, perhaps more than all others, recognized the dialectical quality of objects in consumer society. He recognized how we use them to extend ourselves, to create individual appearances, and also how they use us, how they acquire social meaning as a signaling system in which we almost seem to be props for them, rather than vice versa. The object's value, or significance, takes on meaning independent of any predetermined reality.

Material objects have always had a role to play in human affairs. Fernand Braudel, the great student of material culture, demands that we not scorn those accouterments of the everyday: food, fashion, housing, decor, and so on.[4] It is in and through them that we live, that the economy works, and that the society manifests itself. The objects of the everyday reflect the vitality of society, its energies and its ambitions.

Objects help make appearances; they are there to be read. For Charles Horton Cooley, they are implicated in the sense we have of our own identities, based, in part, on how we think we look to others. This "looking-glass self," as Cooley termed it, is no simple matter. It is no wonder he turned to the example of that master of reading appearances, namely, Sherlock Holmes, to explain it. As Cooley wrote, Holmes says that "six persons take part in every conversation between John and Thomas: 1. The real John, known only to his Maker. 2. John's ideal John, never the real one and often very unlike him. 3. Thomas's ideal John. And, of course, three Thomases. The matter is really more complicated," said Cooley, "and one would not need to go beyond every-day experience to find at least twelve persons participating, six on each side."[5] Appearances have never been a simple matter: reading them, never—except perhaps for Holmes—"elementary."

What's critical *now* is that the relationship of subject and object is changing. Increasing emphasis is being placed on identities based on appearances, rather than on other, more durable, criteria. As moderns we are, as Italian sociologist

Francesco Alberoni said, in love with change. We desire the freedom perpetually to create ourselves anew: to fall in love with each other, to fall in love with ourselves, our beauty makeovers, and even career "makeovers," as the magazines call them.[6] The more traditional criteria out of which identities were constructed, such as family, religion, neighborhood, community, nation, these are of less significance for the modern man or woman. Instead, we go by appearances; we follow fashion. As Baudelaire recognized, fashion is the essence of modernity: it places the transitory above the everlasting, it frees individuals to present themselves as they please, irrespective of any prior ascribed identities.[7]

If there is a recognized tension between individual passions and a social good, recognized, that is, at least since Plato, then objects and their advertisements glorify the individual passions at the expense of the social. They thus contribute to a decline in the legitimacy and efficacy of those social institutions that bind us together. Advertising itself is not the prime mover in this process; rather, it is joined to other forces in the creation of modern society. It helped create our brave new world of comfort and desire. It provided new things to buy, new things to do, new products to savor and services to enjoy. These freed us from much dull, repetitive, and heavy labor. These also fed our dreams.

But with the emphasis on individual comfort, ease, and self-expression, the claims of other people became only faintly heard by the mass. Richard Sennett calls it "the fall of public man" and traces the process of individual and familial isolationism back to the end of the nineteenth century and the retreat from the challenges of modern society.[8] Christopher Lasch labels the current manifestation "the culture of narcissism."[9] Indeed, the "me generation" of the 1970s still seems to have difficulty conceiving and acting in support of the greater "we." Even political scientist Alex Inkeles, who has spent much of his life studying paths toward modernity, occasionally despairs when he considers where modernity has led the nations. In defining a postmodern mentality, he writes, "by postmodern we mean being increasingly oriented to passive rather than active roles; ready to surrender personal autonomy to collective control; suspicious or defeatist about most forms of science; seeking mystical experience or release from boredom through drugs or violence; hostile to any sort of fixed schedule; skeptical about the payoff from personal or social planning. So marked are some of these tendencies, and so much at variance with the main elements of the modernity syndrome," says Inkeles, summing up, "that they might more accurately be described as antimodern."[10]

Advertising, in its own fashion, works to encourage some of these tendencies. It encourages a certain passivity and lack of involvement, as the play of appearances takes over the work of social relations. It offers a release from boredom not through drugs but through products that promise, "And suddenly, nothing will be the same." It says that we should not mind its presence in our homes, for we invite it in every time we subscribe to newspaper or magazine or turn on the television. We should not mind the way its jingles run through our minds.

It is the very state of inattention in which we receive advertising's messages that accounts for much of their effectiveness. As sociologist Michael Schudson argues, advertising catches us in a state of relaxation, reading the Sunday paper or unwinding evenings in front of the television set.[11] It catches us when we are too young to have the critical faculties with which to judge its promises or evaluate its effects. It presents a world of fun and adventure, where we triumph over every adversity. Who needs the hard work, the "fixed schedule," the careful "personal or social planning" of which Inkeles speaks, when good times are assured with every bottle of soda pop and every visit to McDonald's? The world of advertising appeals to the child in us, who looks for pleasure and excitement, who neither knows nor cares about adult responsibilities. When it does deal with serious problems, such as debilitating illness or the death of a breadwinner, it always has the ready solution in a wonder medicine or insurance policy. Even in its solution to the nation's drug epidemic, advertising offers a "quick fix." The message is clear: "Just say no." But even public service advertising can not solve social issues by reducing them to personal problems.[12]

Besides being about appearances, advertising is also about gender. Gender is part of its social structure and its psychology. Gender conditions our response to what we see and helps us decide what to buy.

As historian Roland Marchand has shown, during the critical years from 1920 to 1940 the advertiser was the adman. Although advertising offered some opportunities to women, more than many other businesses in these decades, women were largely ghettoized in jobs with little executive authority. Many, for instance, were copywriters, where they were told to contribute their "feminine viewpoint." The creator of advertising was usually a man, but its target, the consumer, was usually a woman. The relationship between the two was depicted as one of power. Either the adman was shown as being able to control her moves absolutely, as he would a pawn on a chess board, or he was in her power, subservient and obedient to her every whim.[13] In the latter case, she was to be respected for her buying power, primarily, but possibly also for her intelligence and/or taste. The imagery of male advertiser and female consumer continues. As successful advertiser, David Ogilvy wrote in 1963, "The consumer isn't a moron; she is your wife. You insult her intelligence if you assume that mere slogan and a few vapid adjectives will persuade her to buy anything. She wants all the information you can give her."[14]

As Thorstein Veblen correctly perceived, consumption has been defined as women's work in this country ever since women achieved their own "separate sphere." Conspicious consumption emerged as the explicit task and life's work of the wife, who demonstrated through her buying power the wealth of her mate. He could not devote his time to shopping, insofar as he needed to keep up the appropriate class and masculine appearance of seriousness by working at some "honorific" endeavor, rather than fully indulging himself in consumption and a life of leisure.[15]

In the 1920s this gender role division between production (male) and consumption (female), was used by advertisers to justify their profession and to raise it in the public eye. One 1925 advertisement in *Life* shows a hard-working husband initially angered by his wife's demands for a new washing machine. But then on reflection he realizes "that it's advertising that makes America hum. It gives ginks like me a goal. Makes us want something. And the world is so much the better for our heaving a little harder."[16]

The process of consumption is still seen as women's work. Today, although teenagers dominate *discretionary* spending, if we look at overall purchase of consumer goods we see that women still control some 80 percent of the buying power. But, insofar as consumption is dependent on production (where's the money coming from?), it retains its dependent female quality, whether performed by teenagers, still largely dependent, or by women. The "professional shopper" may take herself seriously; few others would.

Operating underneath the level of structural divisions, the psychology of advertising colors our response to it. This psychology has a gendered quality to it insofar as, as Baudrillard correctly perceived, advertising assumes the role of the female. Consumers think they know what they want; advertisements offer that which they desire. The rational man complains that advertisements manipulate—others, of course, seldom himself. But that is exactly the female role—to manipulate, to beseech, to seduce someone in such a manner that he doesn't know what hit him. She must latch on to his desires, only to cast them back toward him, but this time with a hint of mystery. The product, like the woman, must offer a totally new experience. Thus he or she who will be high-minded, noble, and pure will distrust advertising. For it recognizes weakness and caters to it. It invades the very pretense of independent identity.[17]

Advertising is also gendered in that much of it addresses our physical sense of self, our knowledge of the world gained through our bodies. It addresses our need to articulate our social identities through our physical appearances. As John Berger has argued, men create a sense of identity by extending out from their body, using its and their evident *power* to control objects and others. This we see clearly in advertisements for cigarettes, alcohol, stereos, and, especially, automobiles. Women, by contrast, work with and within the body. The female body communicates not the woman's power over others, but her *presence*, how she takes herself.[18] This in turn is reflected in the great emphasis on decoration of the female body, achieved through fashion and cosmetics.

Advertising is also about rationality and irrationality, which exist in and between gender. It is about being in control and being out of control. These are gender modes, I should emphasize, rather than the definition of discrete male and female attitudes or behaviors. Any particular man or woman may, at a given time, operate in one mode or the other; for example, advertisements may use the male mode for products directed toward liberated women.

The advertisements that interest me in particular are those that combine, and thus present in heightened form, these two significances: gender and appearances. I am primarily interested in advertisements that promise *gender appearances*. Many different products have gender as part of their own image or identity, from cigarettes to snow boots. Research shows that men in particular are loathe to use a product targeted at women.[19] A wide range of products promise that their gender identities will help us achieve gender identities, however complex they may be, and to communicate them to one and all, curious or indifferent.

There are other ways to communicate, to put on appearances, than decorating the self. One can decorate one's home, for example, or buy a bigger and more expensive one. One can adopt a power look in one's office, or take up the hobbies, sports, or even religion that one thinks will make the right impression. There is a complicated iconography attached to all of these, one that we will not be able to include here but that has been examined elsewhere.[20]

Feminists have been much concerned about the importance of appearances, particularly within women's lives. Many feminist writers have argued that how a woman looks largely determines how other people react to her. As Simone de Beauvoir wrote in 1949, "Thus the supreme necessity for a woman is to charm a masculine heart; intrepid and adventurous though they may be, it is the recompense to which all heroines aspire; and most often no quality is asked of them other than their beauty." De Beauvoir goes on, "It is understandable that the care of her physical appearance should become for the young girl a real obsession; be they princesses or shepherdesses, they must always be pretty in order to obtain love and happiness."[21] In similar fashion, Susan Brownmiller has described the importance placed on the appearance of femininity. "'Don't lose your femininity' and 'Isn't it remarkable how she manages to retain her femininity' had terrifying implications. They spoke of a bottom-line failure so irreversible that nothing else mattered."[22]

Considerable empirical evidence supports the view that women *are* judged by their beauty. When a man asks, "What is she like?" what he usually means is, "What does she *look* like?" Beautiful people, men and women, are an especially favored race. According to psychologist Elaine Hatfield, "Most people assume that good-looking men and woman have nearly all the positive traits." Parents shower affection on them as children, teachers respond more to them, and they end up with higher-paying jobs.[23] The old belief that women use beauty to marry up has considerable empirical support.[24] In fact, the only area in which beauty does not seem a great blessing for women is when they try to challenge men on their own sacred ground, the boardroom. In high-powered corporations, a stunning-looking woman seems out of place and does not inspire confidence, although a good-looking man does.[25]

The *beauty role*—the importance of appearing attractive in public, of maintaining standards, of encouraging male attention—becomes a central preoccupation for girls and re-mains a concern for women for much of their lives, if not all their lives. In the spring of 1987, the *New York Times* ran two articles about beauty: one explored the various new beauty products available for girls from five on up, including shampoos, lipsticks, and fragrances; the other was an essay by a woman in her sixties explaining why she had a face lift. She wrote, "Having taken for granted that I was a good-looking woman, I nearly lost it, and I found that I minded like hell, and I am eternally grateful that there was something that the doctor and I could do to defeat inevitability for a few more years."[26]

As suggested above, men too are judged by their appear-ances. Men are judged by whether they project an appearance of power and authority. This power can be physical, as commu-nicated through muscles and broad shoulders in a leather jacket and jeans. Or it can be financial: the perfectly tailored suit on the tall executive. Advertising promises rewards, financial and sexual, for the right manly appearance. One writer goes so far as to argue that "practically all advertising is on behalf of the masculine image, either showing him what kind of status he can hope to attain, or showing a woman what kind of man she can hope to attract."[27] One doesn't have to agree fully with this reductionist statement to realize that it is not only women who are objectified in contemporary society. Rather, the difference between male and female appearances is a question both of kind and degree.

Back in the 1960s women rebelled against being judged solely by appearances, of being treated merely as objects, props in someone else's play. Their protests, against beauty "garbage," beauty pageants, and advertisements they found particularly offensive, made news. They made other women conscious of what they had previously left unquestioned. The whole process of examination and challenge changed their lives.

Today, though, it seems as though nothing ever changed. Butch feminism, now associated with army boots, is definitely out. What is in is looking good, whether in the style of 1950s femininity or in the emphasis on Californian "natural" beauty and health (it takes hard work to be natural). Or one can opt for the punk and make a personal statement against society, while still being part of the wave. *Putting on appearances* is one of the biggest games in town. Advertisements let us in on the game's ever-changing rules.

Why are people, women especially, willing to turn them-selves into objects? Why so much stress on outside appear-ances? Writers on beauty often recognize the ambivalence surrounding this topic. "How *does* beauty influence self-esteem and independence? Is adornment an asset or a liability in achieving equality?" As Rita Freedman comments, "Questions of equal pay or equal rights seem clearer and safer. Equal looks are harder to define."[28]

The very concept of "equal looks" helps bring us to the heart of the problem. Very few people within Western societies are attempting to achieve equal looks. Even in China today beauty is a boom business, no longer perceived as being at odds with Maoist doctrine.[29] What they *are* doing is putting on appearances to make an individual statement within a social discourse. This is a complex, often captivating act. Even former Yale University president A. Bartlett Giamatti, now head of baseball's National League, has been drawn to discoursing on style in clothing and the presentation of the self.[30]

Feminists did succeed in loosening some norms of female appearance and in creating new ones. But they did not destroy the beauty role as such, nor the practices of making up and dressing up, even when dressing down. High-minded though their efforts were, it would have been surprising, stunning even, had they fully succeeded. For, besides being *about* gender and *about* appearances, advertisements are also *about* society. Moreover, they are totally embedded within it. Sociologist Michael Schudson has called advertising "capitalist realism," for its overall affirmation of the capitalist set of values and definition of the good life.[31] Understood as such, advertisements are not a pack of lies, as their adversaries would have it. Rather, they reflect shared understandings of who is desirable, who succeeds, who enjoys life to the fullest, and what it all costs. They show us what we need to get from *A* to *B*, to get laid, to get ahead, to have it made. If we don't succeed in gaining wealth, success, and/or happiness, it can't be due to product failure. It must be person failure; we have not lived up to the advertisements. We, not the product advertised, lack "the right stuff." It was, and is, certainly possible to change these promises and understandings, but to ask women as a whole to ignore them totally is asking them to live apart from society, a path that has been taken only by a small minority.

In telling us about society and reaffirming one set of values, those emphasizing individual happiness and achievement through consumption, advertising draws heavily upon the load of Western culture. Through its particular rhetoric of pun and rhyme, it adds new (commercial) meaning to the old cultural meanings. As a cultural form of its own, advertising develops its own narratives of sex and romance, family and community, failure and success, even of transcendence. It provides rituals and structures occasions. Soon, along with MTV and other popular forms it resembles, it may be our only culture.

Thus advertising is not something to be scorned and quickly dismissed. It is not something we can avoid, even if and when we pretend to ignore it, to rise above it. It is part of our cultural surround. Like fish, we hardly stop to think about the water.

When we do simply accept it, advertising is at its most successful. Its very staying power derives from its ability to mimic the social. As society changes, advertising becomes the happy chameleon, always delighted to don spring's new colors. One of the tasks of this analysis is to examine this cultural mimicry, to understand how the psychology and social impact of advertising derive not from some fund of recondite knowledge based on sophisticated market research, but from us ourselves, the consumers, from our social worlds and our dream worlds. Had the Italian philosopher and cultural historian Giambattista Vico lived today, he would remind us that it is *we* who have made advertising, and so it must be comprehensible to us. If we don't take the time to unravel its meanings, maybe what some theorists feel might happen *will* happen. Maybe advertising will make *us*.

TWO

Madison Avenue:
Method and Madness

To speak of advertising is to speak of consumer society, that plentiful world of goods and services we call our own. The history of its development, like that of the advertising industry, has recently attracted the attention of historians and cultural analysts. The reader interested in a fuller version than can presented here is directed to their texts.[1] My purpose in this chapter is, first, to present an overview, emphasizing the arguments that have been made pro and con, and, second, to outline how advertising images are created, and how they will be analyzed in the following chapters.

Though it may be that people have always desired to have "just a little bit more" of everything, historians find that it was only in the eighteenth century that this dream became a possibility for more than the aristocratic few. Then, new wealth culled in part from overseas possessions and vigorous trade combined with internal reforms to raise the standard of living and make England the first real consumer society. New products emerged: fancy dolls displaying the latest fashions that

dressmakers would then copy for their well-off patrons, new
plants to cultivate and pets, especially dogs and horses, to breed
and, in the latter case, raise. Josiah Wedgwood's pottery works
set a new standard for dinnerware and porcelain figurines, and
textile mills exploited Indian cotton and new dyes to fashion
exciting new fabrics that became all the rage in London and the
countryside.[2] Advertising took two forms: men wearing plac-
ards and announcements in the newspapers. But not everyone
accepted its legitimacy. Some found it peculiar that anyone could
advertise his goods or services, daring to put his name on the
very page that might include that of the Prince of Wales! An
honest merchant, some felt, would not stoop to such advertisements; let word-of-mouth spread by satisfied customers
announce his reputation and provide for his livelihood.[3]

In the nineteenth century the mounting forces of industrialization and urbanization made an ever-wider variety of goods
available to people throughout Europe and even in the relatively
backward former colonies, the United States. Improved trans-
portation, the growth of the railroads in particular, served to
take people out of their small villages and towns to show them a
wider world, to instil new desires. Whereas in the small town
every one had his or her place, largely determined by kin,
church, and occupation, in the large cities each was free to make
his or her own way in life: in short, to dream. Old ideas about
one's proper place or station in life eventually gave way in face
of new desires for an improved living standard. America in
particular glorified the desire of the common man to make it big.
By the end of the century he was encapsulated in the writings of
Horatio Alger, in whose books young lads with names such as
Ragged Dick made it big through a combination of their
relentless honesty and hard work and that one lucky break.
Their success was well earned: it supported the cultural myth of
the American Dream.

For women, becoming beautiful was part of that dream.

Historian Lois Banner calls it the woman's version of the American get-ahead spirit.[4] Fashion and standards of female beauty changed; it was every woman's civic duty—and duty to herself—to keep up with them. The major new department stores that developed in the latter half of the nineteenth century and the early decades of the twentieth—New York's Macy's, Detroit's Hudson's, Chicago's Marshall Field's—legitimated shopping as an activity for women of the expanding middle class. These stores became a respectable destination for women who wanted to get out of the house, to see and be seen. The new stores quickly learned how to cater to their female clientele, adding restaurants where women could relax without fear of being bothered, and incorporated new departments for a range of goods previously never shown under one mighty roof.[5]

The old rural ethic that many people had brought with them from peasant and craft backgrounds in European villages died a hard death. The old emphasis was on saving and thrift. The new emphasis was on spending and consumption. Perhaps the most difficult sales job for advertising lay in its convincing people that it was not a sign of a dissolute character or an impoverished pocketbook to buy on credit. In fact, advertisements argued in the 1910s and 1920s, it was the *modern* thing to do. It showed one's faith in oneself and in the future. Credit was patriotic and it was economical. It supported nation and capitalism. It provided the exciting new durables: the new refrigerators, gas ovens, and vacuum cleaners ("Hoovers"). It made living clean. It made life fun.

It was in the 1920s that advertising came of age. Before long, it gained considerable sophistication in marketing a wide range of goods and services: cigarettes, mouthwash, cosmetics, alcohol, automobiles, insurance, encyclopedias. Advertising men became the archetypal modern men: always on the forefront of change, always coming up with something new to sell whatever else was new.[6] As James R. Adams, one of the founders of the advertising agency MacManus, John & Adams Inc., advised young men, "Advertising calls for a constantly curious mind, eager and alert. If you are a conservative and prefer to have things as they are, you can easily get trampled in advertising. Change is the only constant with which we have to deal."[7]

Today, advertising is established fact and major industry. It has its own folklore—witness the rash of advertising histories and confessions—and its own folk heroes—Albert Lasker, David Ogilvy, William Bernbach, now Hal Riney. It is played as art, as science, as craft, and even, according to one advertiser, as witchcraft. "Advertising is the witchcraft of the twentieth century. It has its incantaions, its how-to recipes, . . . its priests and priestesses, its temple whores and secret languages."[8]

It is also like fortune telling. It is the art of looking in crystal balls and telling people who they are, who they might be. Advertising had become one of the means through which we develop a modern sense of self, one perpetually open to change. Social historian T. J. Jackson Lears believes that the destruction of the old bases of identity mentioned above (kin, church, village, occupation) left a void that the new consumer society filled with advice on topics such as self-improvement, "selling oneself," "making friends and influencing people," developing an attractive personality (in contrast to the nineteenth-century emphasis on "character").[9] Would-be advertising men are advised that the one word consumers never tire of is *me*. Advertisers simply tell them who that "me" is, and how to make it ever more attractive, comfortable, exciting, appealing.

To do this, advertisers must do more than communicate information on a product. They must communicate *image*. Their task is somehow to position a product within a market of competing goods and to aim it toward an identifiable population. They must give it a personality. As Roy Bostock, president of the Benton & Bowles advertising agency said, "We call it giving a product a place to live. . . . We try to find a way of articulating to the consumer the benefits of the product or service—a rationale for buying it. Then, and very importantly, we need to give a unique character to the product among its competitors."[10]

As the advertisement slides into our mind and finds a place, as Bostock says, for the product to live, is it committing an act of terror or of service? Is it manipulating us or merely allowing us to dream? Since its origins, advertising has had its critics and defenders.

Among those who attack advertising, some argue that it simply adds to the cost of the product, in some cases very substantially. Advertising does not come cheap. Major agencies have total billings well into the billions; a major account, such as Burger King, may bring in $200 million. The ingredients in perfume, for example, account for only a fraction of its cost to the consumer, who is also paying for expensive packaging and advertising. Advertisers have a hard time showing that advertising directly accounts for increased sales. Rather, the sales of one advertised product often rise at the expense of another, and sometimes unadvertised products do very well indeed.

If advertising can't prove direct economic benefits to the producer who pays for it, critics argue that it may have indirect economic benefits. For Stuart Ewen, advertising arose in the early twentieth century as a powerful means through which the demands of the working class could be subverted. It was a deliberate and successful attempt to support capitalism by changing people's consciousness of themselves as workers, thereby defusing political demands and potential disruption. Workers became consumers with new desires for products and less awareness of their real position within the labor force.[11]

Other analysts question Ewen's argument. Michael Schudson, for one, finds three problems with it. First, the busi-

nessmen Ewen cites were not "captains of industry" but rather
"corporals of advertising and marketing, trying to make their
case to the business world in terms they [thought would] most
delight it." Second, most advertising was directed not at the
working class but at the affluent middle class; and, third, new
research shows that the 1920s working class did not share in the
growing affluence and could probably not have afforded many of
the products advertised. "One's psychological hunches can then
work either way—either this would lead the workers to work
harder to be able, one day, to join in middle class prosperity, or
it would lead to frustration that might trigger political activity."[12]

Many do see advertising as manipulating people in some
broad fashion, as creating new needs and desires. They find the
informational content of much advertising paltry indeed when
compared with its truckload of symbols and its appeals to a
variety of human motives: status, sex, envy, guilt. Since so
much of advertising operates on the unfocused attention, people
succumb to the product without consciously deciding whether
they truly need or want it. One critic, Wilson Key, has even
argued that advertisers use technological dirty tricks of subliminal seduction to work upon the unconscious mind, but no one,
advertising friend or foe, has been able to substantiate his
specific claims.[13]

The more general claim that advertising manipulates our
desires is more broadly argued and more seriously debated.
Typical of the genre is a column written by Lucy Hughes Hallet
and called, simply "Why Perfume Ads Stink." They stink, in her
opinion, because they present the woman with an ideal of female
attractiveness and tell her, "This is what you ought to be. If you
were more like this you would be more desired, more pam-
pered, happier. Ours is the elixir which will transform you. Buy
it."[14]

Advertising is accused of defining not just new needs but new
values. It makes people believe they can find happiness, even

transcendence, through the purchase of products. It encourages rampant materialism. It makes of us a nation of narcissists and individuals, with no way of communicating with each other except through products.

Advertisers respond to these criticisms in a variety of ways. The first is to insist that their business is by no means so powerful as the critics would have it. If we could so easily manipulate consumers, they say, all advertised products would succeed and we would all be living on easy street. But most new products fail, and many advertisements, even if they catch people's attention, do not make them go out and buy. One recent study, for example, reported that 37 percent of people exposed to magazine advertisements and articles don't understand or comprehend them.[15] Consumers act rationally, advertisers say, and advertisements provide the necessary information for them to make their choices in whatever manner they choose. As Benton & Bowles president Roy Bostock remarks, "The interesting thing to me is that the people who criticize advertising for creating needs never consider themselves as being coerced. It's always somebody else down the street."[16]

Rather than coercing people, advertising gives them what they want: a higher standard of living. From the 1920s when advertising began to become big business, it justified its presence by saying that it inspired men to work harder, to provide for their families, to get ahead. And this motivation kept the wheels of the economy spinning, made for a more productive nation and a more affluent society. It was Franklin Delano Roosevelt who said, "If I were starting life over again, I am inclined to think that I would go into the advertising business in preference to almost any other. . . . The general raising of the standards of modern civilization among all groups of people during the past half century would have been impossible without the spreading of the knowledge of higher standards by means of advertising."[17]

Sometimes their defenses took on a religious tone and

imagery. In a best-selling book in the 1920s, adman Bruce Barton suggested that if Jesus were alive he would be in advertising, since he was so good at selling people on his ideas. In a 1958 book based on his thirty years in advertising, James Adams also used biblical language clearly suggesting that America was the Promised Land:

> America is the land of opportunity—but how few have taken advantage of it! Up and down this land of ours are millions who have no idea what a full, well-ordered American life is like. Milk and honey flow all around them—crying to be eaten and drunk—but they live oblivious, these countless millions. . . . A bubbling fountain is in their own back yard, and they sit miserable with thirst.[18]

Adams went on to note that various social and governmental agencies were concerned with these unfortunates, and that was as it should be. "But," he argued, "if any great and permanent good is ever done for these millions, it will not be done through social service or through agencies administering financial welfare. It will be done through organized business. It will be done by creating products at such a low cost that they can be made available to the financially under-privileged, and by then educating these people to take advantage of their new-made opportunities."[19]

Materialism could work magic; it could change peoples' minds. The counterexample was Russia, where politics had changed peoples' minds—but, in the advertisers' opinion—in the wrong direction! Still, even the sullen Soviets would be possible subjects for the advertisers' appeals. As Adams said, "If our government could place one copy of *Life, Look* and *The Saturday Evening Post* into the hands of every living Russian— and could make certain that they were read from cover to cover—there would be more trouble in Russia than the nation has seen since the revolution." Driving the point home, Adams declared, "The advertisements would do the trick."[20]

To accusations of encouraging materialism, then, many advertisers answer, "Guilty as charged," some with more finesse than Adams. Materialism is, after all, what advertising is all about: selling products. As advertiser Edward Buxton commented, "It also sells services, but critics have not yet come to complain about an excess of services, which in fact represent about 40 percent of expenditures and are growing fast. It is the excess of products that rankles most. . . ."[21] Biting the bullet, Buxton continues:

> Our economy is loaded with unnecessary, expendable, nonutilitarian, nonnutritious, useless gadgets, widgets, face creams, nostrums, gimcracks, and what have you. Who is to decide whether people should make them or whether people should buy them? After all, some 37 percent of the median-income family's earnings are discretionary, that is, money not needed for basic food, clothing, and shelter. What should people do with this money? Why shouldn't they do what they wish with it?[22]

On this point Buxton is seconded by David Ogilvy, also founder of his own agency. Specifically addressing the question "Does advertising make people want to buy products they don't need?" Ogilvy argues:

> If you don't think people need deodorants, you are at liberty to criticize advertising for having persuaded 87 percent of American women and 66 percent of American men to use them. If you don't think people need beer, you are right to criticize advertising for having persuaded 58 percent of the adult population to drink it. If you disap-

prove of social mobility, creature comforts, and foreign travel, you are right to blame advertising for encouraging such wickedness. If you dislike affluent society, you are right to blame advertising for inciting the masses to pursue it.

If you are this kind of Puritan, I cannot reason with you. I can only call you a psychic masochist . . . .

Ogilvy concludes by recalling how the father of the labor movement in England, John Burns, "used to say that the tragedy of the working class was the poverty of their desires. I make," said Ogilvy, "no apology for inciting the working class to desire less Spartan lives."[23]

Finally, it is worth hearing from one advertiser who admits to the occasional doubt about his profession. John Straiton writes, "Earning a living by selling things and influencing attitudes as I do, my assessment of my craft goes from an abysmal low, as it did when I read *The Selling of the President 1968* by Joe McGinniss and I found I knew one of the people involved, to moderate heights, as when I introduced a worthwhile product like Johnson & Johnson J-cloths, helped people lose weight with Metrecal, or helped make Canadians become a little less wasteful in their use of energy." Zeroing in on the question, he asks himself—and us—"Is selling Betsy Wetsy entirely wrong?"

Besides bringing inordinate joy to a little girl for a few dripping moments, I have also contributed a mite to the saleslady's salary in Eaton's store. I have helped create a moment of work for the person at the plastic machine moulding the Betsy Wetsy, and another portion of piece-work for the skilled worker boring the hole for the wet to come out and for the checker who makes sure the hole is well and truly bored.

Straiton also sees himself as having helped the chainsaw operator who cut down the tree, the workers who constructed the box, the printer and ink-maker responsible for the packaging, the trucker who transported the product, the television station workers who benefited by having his advertisement pay for their programs (and salaries), and the various people in the department store that sold it. Then he concludes with a most interesting observation:

> One might comment that Betsy Wetsy and indeed the commercialization of Christmas itself, might easily be done away with and none the worse. Perhaps so. But most of life is not directly involved with basic nutrients, procreation, and avoiding freezing to death is, to some degree, in the same category as Betsy Wetsy, from the automatic gear shift to the Sistine Chapel ceiling. Not essential, but they do improve the quality of life. [24]

Is, as Straiton suggests here, a plastic doll that wets its pants fundamentally in the same category as Michelangelo's masterful painting of the Sistine Chapel? In this book, I am arguing that advertising draws heavily on the cultural lode of Western civilization. But are advertising and the products advertised essentially the same as such recognized high points of art and civilization? Do they now serve us (and serve us well), both as the descendents and inheritors of the civilization we have lost, or progressed beyond?

While we cannot place a price tag on the Sistine Chapel, we can put a price on a Van Gogh, namely, forty million dollars. Insofar as we can put a price on both Betsy Wetsy and Van Gogh's sunflowers, and insofar as they are both not concerned with mere survival, does that, as Straiton suggests, put them "to some degree, in the same category"?

This cultural reductionism points the way to the heart of the matter. Advertising is not, as its sharpest critics suggest, a wicked manipulator of an innocent public. Nor is it, as its defenders argue, the mere servant of society. It is, rather, that, as the literature of consumerism, it is not disinterested. It does not exist for our amusement or our edification. It exists to sell goods. It has but one happy ending, more sales for the producers, fatter accounts for the agency.

In pursuit of this ending, advertising makes everything equivalent, mere grist for the mill, so much subject material: Betsy Wetsys, Sistine Chapels, the Renaissance, diet sodas, space travel, hair dryers, mother love, face creams. All are but images and ideas, just so much "stuff." It is this pretension that creates a certain unease among those who hold other values, which they see devalued and coopted by advertising. Consumerism is a fun game, but when it becomes the only game we know how to play, something is lost: some alternate way of understanding, appreciating, and valuing the nonessential products of human production.

In the chapters that follow we will examine this process of cooptation and see how the game of advertising is played on us and through us, through our purchases, our existence as discernible and much-studied "markets." Let us first, however, consider some of its ground rules. The first of these concerns the necessity of creating an image, the art of positioning the product.

Creating an Image

One thing critics and defenders agree on is that products are not sold simply on the basis of what they are, but rather also on the basis of what image they project. Products must be positioned within the array of competing goods. They must be aimed at an identifiable segment of the market and must achieve identity themselves.

Research has come to play an increasingly important part in this process. In the 1950s, as advertisers grew increasingly sophisticated in handling statistics and market research, in testing out possible ideas, some saw little role for the creative minds, the copywriters and artists, who were there simply to execute the campaigns selected by the research. But then in the 1960s there was a creative revolution, with new blood challenging the advertising profession's received wisdom about the primary of research. Street-smart ethnics, very often Jews (as copywriters) and Italians (as artists) created campaigns with humor and the common touch. As an example of this new creativity, consider how William Bernbach created a new campaign for Levy's, a major Brooklyn bakery. Bernbach, himself from Brooklyn, knew that the product was a good one. But sales were down and he was called in. As fellow advertiser Edward Buxton recalls the incident:

> Sitting in the small office of the bakery on his first visit to Levy, Bill asked, "Why isn't your bread selling? Have you cut the quality, changed anything?"
>
> "No," the baker said. "Same bread. Best we can make. People just don't like it anymore, I guess."
>
> Bernbach then asked, "You make a lot of different kinds of bread—which one do you think is the very best one? The one people should hear about?"
>
> "The Jewish rye," was the immediate reply. "It's beautiful."
>
> "That's funny," Bernbach said. "You never mention Jewish rye in your advertising. Never once. Why?"
>
> The head of the company shrugged. "Well, you know,—it's Jewish. Maybe some people might think— they are anti-Semitic—or something."
>
> Bernbach thought for a minute. Then said, "It's your best bread—sell it. With a name like Levy—people are going to know you're Jewish." And Bill proceeded to tell

him how the advertising should be handled. The results
were the now famous poster ads, "You don't have to be
Jewish to love Levy's ryebread," featuring blacks, Italians,
Chinese, Indians, etc.

As Buxton comments, "Bill Bernbach understood ordinary
people. And how to talk to them."[25] He effectively used a gentle
humor and honesty about the product to position it among the
many competing brands, making it attractive to a wide range of
potential consumers.

Today, the dominant image has changed from the street-
smart urban to homespun small town. But the magic touch,
whatever form it takes, still has to be there. As a competitor
said regarding the very successful commercials San Francisco
adman Hal Riney did for Gallo's Bartles and Jaymes wine
coolers, "Entrepreneurs like Ernest Gallo are drawn to a guy
like Riney who understands how to talk to audiences in their
own language. . . . His marketing people probably all argued
against Bartles and Jaymes, but Gallo had the guts to trust
Riney, and the instinct to know that his closing line—'Thank you
for your support'—would resonate not just in Riney's mind, but
in everybody else's too."[26]

Bernbach and Riney make it look easy. But finding the right
image, an image that will sell, is a difficult business. Research
can only point the way. It cannot come up with the answer. As
David Ogilvy writes, "How do you decide what kind of image to
build? There is no short answer. Research cannot help you
much here. You have actually got to use judgment." He remarks
upon the "increasing reluctance" among some executives to use
their judgment, relying instead too much on research: "They
use it as a drunkard uses a lamp post, for support rather than for
illumination."[27] Advertisers with creative reputations such as
Ogilvy and Bernbach believe that research, though useful,
cannot answer some of the key questions, such as whether

someone who can identify an advertising slogan will actually buy the product. As one advertiser said, "The thing that intrigues me is that everyone thinks the advertising business is so sophisticated and that we have all sorts of research. We always laugh at that. We're working on something and come up with a dumb idea and laugh. Things happen so simply. In a lot of cases you don't need years of experience. If you are a good lateral thinker and approach it from a different way then you can present it to the consumer."[28] Ogilvy calls this creative process "a groping experimentation with ideas, governed by intuitive hunches and inspired by the unconscious."[29] James Adams considers all of life as grist for the creative mind.[30]

Some summarize this creative process as comprising the four steps of assimilation (of information), gestation (thinking it over), inspiration (eureka!), and evaluation (will it sell in Dubuque?).[31] It is in the stage of inspiration that creativity reveals itself. How does this happen?

Arthur Koestler would argue that creative ideas come from the joining of two different planes of thought or reality, and the ability of the individual mind, like a spark, to jump the gap between them.[32] If this is a fair metaphor for creative thinking, the next question is, What are the relevant planes to be jumped? In other words, what is the material the creative staff has to work with and from?

One plane is provided by the product itself. This is where the creative mind informs itself of all relevant aspects of the product that might help position it apart from the competition. Existing image, relative price, reliability, name recognition, distinctive characteristics, or targeted market are only a few of the dimensions commonly taken into account. Thus the first step the creative staff faces is to familiarize themselves with all aspects of the product and its position in the market.

With this first plane of product characteristics in mind, the creative staff must now somehow leap imaginatively to a second plane if the result is to be a successful, striking advertisement. What provides this second plane, the verbal and visual connections that will henceforth be associated with the product?

This second plane could be almost anything. The inspiration might come from a play with language, from the simple act of contradiction with product characteristics, as in "You don't have to be Jewish to love Levy's ryebread." Much of the rhetoric of advertising plays upon irony, paradox, and wild punning.

Many of the images created by advertisers draw upon well-known elements of Western culture. Social critic John Berger is among those who see advertisements as the inheritors of Western high art: "It is a mistake to think of publicity supplanting the visual art of post-Renaissance Europe; it is the last moribund form of that art." He continues by commenting on the essentially "nostalgic quality of advertising insofar as it can not provide its own standards. Any reference to quality must be based on tradition, on what has been accepted as luxury in other settings, other centuries." Advertising, he writes, "would lack both confidence and credibility if it used a strictly contemporary language."[33]

And yet advertisers seem increasingly willing to draw upon the images not just of high culture but of popular culture to sell their products. One very successful 1987 commercial sold raisins by having raisin models dance to the rock tune "I Heard It Through the Grapevine." Others adopt punk styles in visuals, language, and format. We are coming into a stage where advertising is not simply referring to high culture, but to its own products. George Lois, creator of the famous "I want my Maypo" cereal advertisement, later followed up with "I want my MTV."[34]

It is not simply cultural products citing other cultural products. There's a whole social world out there, heavy with symbolism. Reflecting the world of business, nightgowns become "fashion investments." The world of the military is suggested by frequent reference to "conquests," "revolutions," and "strategies." Female models are posed in government legislatures and corporate board rooms. Women's liberation was not seriously resisted by advertisers. Rather, it presented new material, new frames of reference, new hopes, dreams, and desires to be called upon and served. The advertisement represents the leap between product and society. It suggests that if the woman buys the product, then she will gain access to those realms of activity—leadership in business, politics, the military—from which the majority of women have traditionally been excluded.

Some advertisers find it appropriate to use these new dreams of success to sell products, but others see the traditional images of female culture as being more effective. Their sources lie in tradition, in fairy tales of Cinderellas and Snow Whites, in female folk wisdom, in the very routines and rituals of female sexuality and domesticity. They rely upon the distinctive set of values women create and have created for them. Jessie Bernard has defined love and duty as the two central values defining the ethos of the female world.[35] With much of this traditional world centered on self-sacrifice ("What's a mother for?"), beauty and glamour constitute an important, socially legitimated "time out." As the models in advertisements say, "This I do for me" and "I'm worth it."

To study these advertisements as creative products, we must open our minds to symbolism and imagery just as do their creators, the advertising artists and copywriters. Much of social science research, however, has approached advertisements as if they were perfectly straightforward, void of all cultural and psychological complexity. Content analysis is a long and well-established tradition in social science research. It relies upon categories and counting, checks and doublechecks through multiple scorers. It has been viewed as our most reliable method of obtaining the truth from documents ranging from works of fiction to newspapers, from television serials to advertisements.

My purpose is not to attack a method that has so clearly proved its worth to social science. In fact, I rely upon it to get an accurate reading of what product types are being advertised in what number in the magazines studied. This provides an important sense of the components being presented as crucial to "putting on appearances," and it provides the basis for comparisons among the different women's magazines and between women's and men's magazines (see Appendix).

But I would suggest that content analysis has certain limitations, especially in dealing with advertisements so often involving elements of play and fantasy. Content analysis assumes the relevant piece of data to be the individual advertisement, which is to be coded according to the pretested schema by a panel of coders. But consider a shoe advertisement. It may feature simply a shoe against a blank background, with the manufacturer's name written below. With such evident content, it might score low or be coded as simple presentation of name and product. In truth, that individual advertisement draws upon the body of advertisements. It depends upon the woman reader's previous exposure to all such products and myriad other advertisements, for shoes and other beauty goods. The individual advertisement signifies far more than is immediately apparent. The sum of such advertisements is of greater significance and impact than the parts.

Following the same line of reasoning, content analysis usually counts all advertisements equally. This is based on a dubious assumption that all have equal impact (or on the inability to find a system for weighting them). Advertisers themselves give out awards for "best advertisements," clearly signaling that they believe that some advertisements make more of an impact than do others. Market researchers study the different appeals of advertising approaches. Consumers remember certain campaigns and forget others. Despite the assumptions inherent in content analysis, advertising producers, market researchers, and many consumers would agree that all advertisements are not equal in impact. Some are more convincing, make more of a statement, appeal more to readers, and encourage them to buy the product more than do others.

To some extent, content analysis as a method displays certain affinities with market research. Both are highly controlled comparisons of specific advertisements, both involve much counting and testing across populations and are increasingly subject to statistical manipulations. As we approach advertising as a subject, we would do well to keep in mind the advertisers' suspicion of such research: using it where appropriate, where, as here, product types can be counted with some degree of accuracy, but using other, more interpretative methods, to study the meanings behind the numbers.[36]

In doing this I have used what Umberto Eco might recognize as an "aberrant code."[37] Instead of assimilating advertisements semiconsciously, as a consumer, I have sought to apply insights from a wide reading in social and feminist theory. As the reader will have already noted, I have been influenced by semiologists such as Roland Barthes and by poststructuralists such as Jean Baudrillard.

For Baudrillard, the "system of objects" is a complex one indeed. To understand it, and them, one must be familiar with a number of different "codes"—meaning systems like languages in which the objects function as signs, signifying something beyond their simple existence. He calls the first of these codes the *phantasmataic logic* derived primarily from the vocabulary of psychoanalysis, "its identifications, projections, and the entire imaginary realm of transcendence, power and sexuality." The second, the *differential social logic,* is concerned primarily with consumption as a means to status and prestige. The third code, or logic, may be less obvious. This is the logic of symbolic

exchange, what Baudrillard terms the *sacrificial logic* of consumption, involving such terms as gift, expenditure, luxury,
mutilation.[38] In defining this third logic, Baudrillard shows
intellectual indebtedness to Georges Bataille, surrealist and
anthropologist manqué. For Bataille, the whole emphasis in
social theory on *saving,* on rational action plotted by the rational
person in pursuit of self-interest, has to be balanced by an
awareness of what he calls *dépens,* or expenditure. *Dépens*
includes all the ways through which people and societies are
wasteful of resources, all the ways in which they do more than is
necessary, or even beneficial, for survival or progress. *Dépens*
implies a letting loose, a spending of excess resources and
energies in symbolic gestures. As we will see, many advertisements display such symbolic excess, whether in the form of
luxury or the detailed attention to body decoration.[39]

This code consists not of separate pieces of data with
meaning obvious to any trained coder, but as complex signs with
subtle contents that may sometimes evoke different referents.
One television commercial showed a pretty young woman at the
end of a long corridor. As the camera zoomed in, she looked
straight into its lens and said, dramatically, "I have a license
. . . ." What did she have a license for? To kill, like James
Bond? To steal, to drive? No, she had a license to *eat* (diet
food). Whatever the guess, the central idea was one of breaking
social restrictions and boundaries, an idea discussed in Chapter
Five.

Feminists would have a lot to say about young women who
are and are not allowed to eat. My reading of advertisements is
informed by feminist theory and study. Advertisers from the
early decades of the century on have presented themselves as
performing a tremendous service to humankind. Feminists have
repeatedly asserted that advertisers' consistent placing of
women in either homemaker or glamour roles represents a
*dis*service to womankind.[40]

Recent writings by feminists have attacked the broad issues of femininity and beauty.[41] My work builds upon their insights but differs by emphasizing the whole process of putting on appearances *today*. Rather than exploring beauty across the ages and women as performing a separate and distinctive beauty role, I examine the extent to which beauty imagery is tied into broader cultural currents, symbols, and processes. This, I argue, is precisely what makes beauty imagery so enduring. It is part of what makes the process of "objectification" so difficult, if not impossible, to resist.

The reader will also find reference to many other theorists who have commented upon modern society in its many manifestations: Marx, Freud, Weber, Simmel, among others. The work of such anthropologists as Victor Turner on ritual and Mary Douglas on the symbolic exchange of goods is also critical for an understanding of the role of objects and appearances in everyday life. Thus I don't believe we need a separate feminist theory to understand such cultural formations as advertising; rather, feminism forms a critical part of social theory and adds to its discourse, enabling it—and us—to read more deeply into social life, and here, in particular, to see the role that we ourselves play in this world of appearances.

Magazines Surveyed

The following analysis explores these connotations as it examines advertisements garnered from leading women's beauty and glamour magazines and a smaller sample of men's magazines. The data from the preliminary sample of women's magazines were collected from 1979 to 1981, and those from a follow-up six-month sample, from January through June 1987, when data from the men's magazines were also collected. The women's magazines were selected because they had high circulations and represented a range of markets: affluent women, teenagers, young career women, and black women.

Vogue, with a 1986 circulation of 1.3 million, is aimed at the affluent upper middle- and upper-class woman. Founded back in 1892, *Vogue* owes its longevity at least in part to its appearance of sophistication and class. In her survey of women's magazines, Connie Miller describes *Vogue*'s distinctive approach: "Instead of family hostels, *Vogue* describes grand hotels; picnic punch recipes tend to be omitted in favor of connoisseur wine recommendations. While far from being feminist oriented, the magazine has remained sensitively in tune with the changes affecting women's lives, offering both regular departments and feature articles that reflect transition and diversity." Articles by prominent authors are also featured.[42]

With its circulation of 2 million, *Glamour* has the largest circulation of the magazines selected. It is no newcomer to newsstands, having been founded in 1939. Its success is due in part to its ability to cover the range of topics of interest to young women: beauty, health, fitness, travel, entertainment, parents, college, work. It also features surveys of readers on many topical issues, and a "How To Do Anything Better Guide" gives advice on everything from how to get tar off your shoes to how to keep a job. Miller writes, "Like other publications of its type, *Glamour* pays lip service to issues the women's movement has raised, an emphasis which—for its two million subscribers— appears to be perfectly satisfactory."[43]

Self, Glamour's physically fit and health-conscious younger sister (founded 1979), has a circulation of just over 1 million. As Miller writes, "Its title and approach indicate *Self*'s intended audience—the 20- to 40-year old, independent, professional woman. Marriage and the family, while not entirely absent, take a backseat to concerns of interest to women as individuals." There is practical advice on beauty and health care; believable role models tell the reader how success can be achieved. *Self* represents one of a breed of new, post-1970s magazines with a slightly different philosophy and outlook from their older coun-terparts, one with more emphasis on fitness than cosmetic beauty, less on getting a man and more on having it all. *"Savvy* and *Working Woman* are for the executive; perhaps it is *Self*'s attempt to appeal to a broader range of women who work that accounts for its significantly higher circulation."[44] Recently, *Self* announced that it would place more emphasis on health and nutrition, including fitness, than on fitness per se. Its new editor, Valorie Griffith Weaver, believes that readers think it is "easier to do something in your kitchen than to go out and run for an hour."[45] Expect more advertisements for food, fewer for running shoes.

Cosmopolitan is another thing altogether. Like *Vogue,* it has been around a long time (founded 1886). Unlike *Vogue,* it has gone through several incarnations. Its latest, and highly suc-cessful (circulation nearly 2.4 million), is described by Miller as "daring traditionalism." "Describing a recent trip to the Cannes Film Festival, Brown [Helen Gurley Brown, editor] says, 'It is so tacky, so marvellous, so irresistible, no wonder I badger my husband to take me.' " Departments include articles and fea-tures, food and decorating, fiction, celebrities, beauty, and fashion. *Cosmopolitan* favors quizzes and surveys ("Are you in Charge of Your Life?") and combines some interest in careers with a great interest in sex ("The Bliss of Semipublic Sex," "Having a Ball with Mr. Wrong"). It also includes an agony column, horoscopes, health, travel, dieting tips, and book and movie reviews.[46]

Essence, circulation 75,000, is the leading magazine for black women. "When you miss *Essence,* you miss you." Founded in 1970, *Essence* is aimed at the young to middle-aged and fairly affluent who are interested in fashion, family, *and* career. With plentiful articles on the expected topics, it also frequently publishes more provocative material especially concerned with the political position of blacks in America.[47]

According to its own publicity, *Seventeen* is "where the girl becomes the woman." Founded in 1944, its circulation in 1986 was just over 1.5 million. Miller accurately describes its image as "fresh-faced" and "well-behaved . . . there is no sleaze here!" It publishes the standard topics of a women's magazine, but they are geared toward middle-class high school girls: fashion, health, beauty, family, careers, plus advice on college and how to handle boys. There are the usual entertainment columns and usually a short story.[48]

There are many other girls' and womens' magazines stressing the beauty role and selling products to help women accomplish it. One might mention in passing *Mademoiselle, YM* (formerly *Young Miss*), *Harper's Bazaar, New Woman,* and *Savvy.*

In contrast, men's beauty magazines are few and far between. One thinks of the well-established *GQ,* but even its circulation is only 446,000—in contrast to *Glamour*'s 2 million. It's not that men do not buy magazines. They do. They buy *Playboy* (circulation 4.1 million), *Penthouse* (3.8 million), *Sports Illustrated* (2.7 million), and *Hustler* (1.5 million).[49]

Putting on appearances, whether seen as reflecting vanity or virtue, has been considered a primarily female interest or activity. But if modern society works to emphasize appearances over identity, style over substance, perhaps what once pertained only to women will increasingly shape the lives of both men and women. Perhaps, also, in this sense, the identity assigned to women is more modern than that assigned to men, to the extent to which the former is based upon a complicated if immediate presentation of identity through appearances. Walter Benjamin thought so, seeing in woman a "baroque elaboration of body parts."[50]—a theme echoed in advertisements for makeup "for eyes, lips, cheeks, and nails." This is a game in which we are all becoming players, adept or inept. Men too can learn from women's experiences.

THREE
The Voices of Authority

Consumers are constantly being told what to do. They are praised for their efforts, reinforced for their interest in beauty, and encouraged to further striving toward their beauty ideal. They are scolded for their failings, for their ignorance and their sloth, for not keeping up with the latest wisdom or for not carrying out to the full the expectations of the beauty role. They are, in brief, kept in the position of the child. The voices of authority hold them in line.

Beauty speaks with several voices. The first, perhaps the most common, is anonymous. "This is the summer to paint your knees!" "Now is the time to get a really new haircut!" Who says? Roland Barthes identifies this as the *passive imperative* voice, through which women are told what they absolutely must do, but they are not told by whom.[1] Advertisements assume their own authority, their own mystique. They speak as though they had expert knowledge; more significantly, they imply that this knowledge of theirs is disinterested. But of course it is not. It is very much in their interest, the interest of the advertisers and the manufacturers, that women accept it unquestioningly and buy the advertised product unthinkingly. "Is your make-up keeping up with the needs of your skin?" . . . "Look to new *Fashion Color Texture* for the finishing touch . . . to your legs!" . . . "Shouldn't you take care of your nails as well as you take care of your skin?"

Female Knowledge

Besides this generalized, anonymous authority, advertising assumes several other voices. The first draws upon the closeness of the mother-daughter relationship. It is nurturing, protective, gently encouraging, and born of experience. It is used exclusively in women's advertisements; in men's advertisements, mother is anathema. It is often found in skin-care advertisements, reminding women, as mother did, to wash their faces and clean their teeth. Good skin habits "will carry you through a lifetime." All it takes is a few "Precious Minutes . . . for a softer, smoother skin.":

> Busy as we all are these days, there are some things we shouldn't neglect. And, if we care about the way we look, skin care is one of those things . . .
> A few minutes is all your skin needs to feel cleaner, fresher, softer. A few Precious Minutes, minutes you won't notice but your skin will.

> Oil of Olay, night and morning, takes only a minute of your day. But once it becomes as much of a habit as getting up and going to bed, it could well be the most important minute of your day. So make a fresh start. Make a resolution that Oil of Olay will be a regular part of your skin-care routine from now on. And you'll never regret it.

Clinique distills the emphasis on habits, instilled by mother, down to the single line of copy, placed above skin-care products and toothbrush: "Twice a day." Manufacturers speak of women who have acquired the beauty "habit." And, insofar as the definition of habit includes unthinking response, born of repetition, they are eager to have their products form part of it. [2]

Recurrent images in these advertisements are of wholesome freshness, softness, innocence, and purity. Vichy milk and lotion appeals to all these when it tells women that "a beautiful day starts with a carefully cleansed skin."

> Just when you've woken, what could be more pleasant to your skin than the softness of a Cleansing milk and the freshness of a Lotion?
>
> First: Vichy Cleansing Milk. it removes and absorbs all impurities, while respecting the natural balance of the skin . . .
>
> Next: the Lotion. it is the freshest and softest way of removing every last trace of Milk . . .
>
> Now, your skin is perfectly clean and feels soft and fresh.

Sometimes, though, when daughter does not listen to this gentle advice, mother has to assume a sterner stance, as in the body lotion advertisement that scolds *"No more excuses"*:

> Many women avoid body lotion.
> Never use it. They have reasons.
>
> They say it's too much trouble.
> Takes so long to sink in. Feels
> sticky. Might damage clothes.
>
> But Greaseless Body Lotion
> from Clinique does none of this . . .

Clinique has ended the problems.
Now, anyone still missing out on
body lotion has no excuse.

If one follows maternal advice, the promise is of continued
childhood, of remaining safe and protected:

Night of Olay's rich emollients penetrate your skin,
creating a nurturing environment similar to the one your
skin had when you were young. Throughout the night,
Night of Olay eases dryness, until tiny wrinkles seem to
fade from view . . .

Night of Olay will take over where mother left off. As one
sleeps, it creates a "nurturing environment," just as mother did
"when you were young." It watches over you, smoothing brow
and skin, until you wake, refreshed, reborn.

In contrast to these advertisements that adopt the maternal
tone implicitly, alternately chiding and encouraging, others use
mother as explicit referent, a point of departure for the
daughter's choices of consumption. Sometimes, mother still
knows what's best for her daughter. The cartoon shows a
college girl opening a large package marked "Handle with Care"
and stuffed full of packages of Sweet 'n Low artificial sweetener:
"Opening the Care package, Mary Agnes finally understood the
depth of her mother's ESP." The very name Mary Agnes
suggests a dutiful daughter (perhaps parochial-school trained?)
who has not yet begun to question mother's wisdom.

Other advertisements suggest that the young woman, now
on her own *should* reevaluate mother's guidelines. New guidelines are, of course, provided in the advertisement. "Did you
think Mom wanted you to use pads forever?" asks the Tampax
advertisement, the accompanying photograph showing attrac-

tive mother with arms protectively folded around grown daughter. The copy explains:

> Do you remember the first time you had this talk with Mom? Well we understand that Mom would first tell you to use pads. That's because her mother probably told her the same thing. But like most Moms, she didn't mean that to be forever. So, if you're still using pads maybe you should reconsider why Tampax tampons might be better.

The hint of revolt in the idea of contradicting mother, suggested above, is also found in, of all things, an advertisement for irons. "Mother told me never buy anything but a GE iron . . . That's why I got a Black & Decker." Here the revolt is quickly resolved and defused:

> Mother and I couldn't see eye to eye on a lot of things—but choosing the best iron wasn't one of them. She believed, and I agreed, there was nothing as good as a GE iron. Today, GE irons are made by Black & Decker. So, that's what I use: Black and Decker.

In other advertisements, though, mother and her opinions are, well, frankly, out of date. "Mother didn't know all the facts of life. (Poor thing.)" says the young blond in the white silk pants outfit, surrounded by four fluffy white kittens. "Mother thought all tampons were the same. She didn't know the facts about Playtex Tampons." In another, particularly cloying, two-page advertisement, we have a black-and-white high school photograph of "Mom" with her bouffant hairdo contrasted with the full-color photograph of daughter with her own trendy look. "What made your mom look this weird . . . can make you look this wonderful."

Clairol Heated Rollers helped make your mom Miss Hot Stuff of the Sixties. They can do the same for you today. With styles Mom never dreamed of . . .

Use them for more body. More volume.

Use them to experiment with a whole new look, or just to make a disobedient curl behave.

And remember, before you call your mom's graduation photo "weird," think what your kids will call yours in the year 2000.

Finally, one deodorant advertisement suggests that, from the daughter's point of view, not only is Mom out of date, she's also over the hill. The teenager explains, "why I need a better roll-on than my mom."

My mom uses an ordinary roll-on. That's OK, but my needs are different . . .

I guess I lead a far more active life, although my mom might disagree. And I seem to keep finding myself in all kinds of exciting situations that could be absolutely ruined by nasty perspiration wetness. I think my mom's a bit past that stage, you know what I mean.

Mother may be past excitement, but she's not past caring. Advertisers rejoice that the population of women who have the beauty habit is growing, with women continuing the habit as they age. Products are positioned within this growing market, such that certain skin-care products are aimed at teenagers, others at women in the lucrative over-thirty-five-year-old market. Even shampoos are now aimed at women over forty, whose hair, presumably, has specific needs.

In many traditional societies older women retired into dark colors and plain faces, and sat in groups clucking over the folly and scandal of young girls. Not so today. Today, women are told they can—and should—be beautiful at any age. Today, it's the young girls who hold the cards, who cluck at their mothers' desperate attempts to get with it and to stay young.

Scientific Knowledge

For such women who no longer have youth on their side, who have long since stopped listening to their mothers, a second voice of authority tells them which products to choose and why. This voice is not born of experience, but of experiment. This is the voice of science. It is associated with the male voice insofar as it speaks the voice of reason and logic, of proven fact:[3]

LOGIC, NOT MAGIC

Dr. George Korkos, the founder of Responsif Company, is an eminent cosmetic surgeon. His world is one of strict logic, a world where roses don't bloom in the desert. And where surgery can't improve the texture of the skin.

The Responsif Age Response System is a cosmetic surgeon's solution, through research, to your desire for younger looking skin. Its exclusive extract infuses your skin with soluble proteins and amino acids, easing fine lines and restoring moisture. It will end *your* search for roses in the desert.

The logic of Responsif. Younger looking skin without magic.

As in the above example, male authority figures—cosmetic surgeons, scientists, doctors—are associated with this voice. They presumably know, the consumer presumably does not. Another example presents a complicated chemical formula, which can only impress the consumer with her relative ignorance:

DR. CHRISTIAAN BARNARD ON
THE QUALITY OF LIFE.

". . . Nothing, as far as I know, has a greater effect on the quality of life than aging, for it affects all of our organs, including the body's largest organ—our skin.

". . . This concern with aging and its impact on the quality of life is the major reason for my involvement with the Schaefer Institute in Switzerland. It was the principal focus of my work there.

"During this period my colleagues and I determined that a specific type of Glycosphingolipid was more abundant in young skin than in older skin.

These efforts were the basis for the development of a complex which contains a specific Glycosphingolipid that we call GSL, expressed as:

$$CH_3 - (CH_2)_{13}CH_2 \diagup\!\!=\!\!\diagdown \overset{\displaystyle OH}{\diagdown} \diagup CH_2 - O - R$$
$$\underset{\displaystyle NH}{\mid}$$
$$CH_3 - (CH_2)_9 - CH = CH - CH_2 - C = O$$

"I believe as a result of these efforts people may be able to significantly improve the quality of their lives."

Here Dr. Christiaan Barnard is presented in the guise of both scientist and humanitarian. It is his concern for the quality of life, associated with his pathbreaking work in heart transplants, rather than any concern with profits, that leads him to experiment in face cream chemistry. Somebody, though, was not taken in, and legally challenged the advertising company with suggesting that Barnard and his Glycosphingolipid could reverse the process of aging. Many other companies have recently come under official scrutiny for the claims they are making on behalf of anti-aging creams.[4]

The authority figure does not have to be male. It is the

language and the tone that matter. An advertisement in *Vogue* shows an attractive female scientist intently staring into her microscope. "This woman has discovered the molecule that helps reverse the visible effects of skin's aging."

> She is bio-chemist Chantal Burison
> Now her discovery and application of the Elasyn cosmetic molecule, the missing link to skin's vital elastin collagen balance, is yours to experience.
> . . . Because of its remarkable qualities and infinitesimal size, the Elasyn cosmetic molecule can actually penetrate the dermis cells—where elastin and collagen are produced—to help restore the important elastin collagen balance.
> Why is this balance so vital to your skin? Biologically, after 25 years of age, elastin production decreases—leaving your skin with less elasticity. The result: lines and wrinkles. The alternative Elasyn Essence.

The consumer stood a better chance with mother. Then she could at least answer back. What can she say to these advertisements? Is she really willing to wager her skin, to call the scientists' bluff, when she cannot necessarily understand their language, much less duplicate their experiments? She is separated from the product, and knowledge of it, by clouds of mystification. The powers claimed for science are reflected in the very names of the products: Clinique, Evidence, Biotherm, Hydrothermal Day Cream, Visible Difference, Traitement B23 Points Vulnerables, Bio-Clear Washing Grains. Helena Rubenstein goes so far as to claim to having developed her own "Science of Beauty." Accordingly:

> The Science of Beauty is a philosophy that we try to apply to everything we do at Helena Rubenstein. Quite

simply, we have been aware since the formation of our company that beauty is no longer a hit-or-miss affair, that by the application of scientific facts we can bring to the world of beauty the benefits of painstakingly researched advances in the field of cosmetic development.

Clinique presents an image of cosmetic table as science lab. Its Clinique computer promises to "take the guesswork out of how to properly care for your skin." The customer does not need FORTRAN to know which products to purchase. Instead, she is instructed to:

Slide knob so that correct answer appears in the window at right.

When all eight questions have been answered, some one background tint will dominate in the answer column.

Match this shade to one of the tints shown below.

This is the key to your Clinique skin type.

If you *always burn* in the sun, you are always a Type I skin.

In case of a tie, the consultant will ask you a tie-breaking question.

The language in these advertisements is new, with its references to science and computers, but the promise is old: to forestall time, to keep people guessing. "With NEW EVI-DENCE your skin can lie about your age." To the black woman, Fashion Fair suggests, "Put your age on hold with Fashion Fair's Fabulous Special Beauty Creme with collagen. . . . Collagen helps your skin cope with lines caused by frowns, smiles, yawns, grins, and squints. Put your age on hold."

Sensitive to charges of quackery, advertisers take pains to demonstrate the seriousness of manufacturers' efforts and the resulting soundness of their products. As one example:

Revivance Biological complex D.P.P. was developed after five years of laboratory testing in France. In a *matter of weeks* it will help diminish the signs and symptoms of aging: correct lack of tone, dryness, flakiness, with a cellular-bonding ingredient.

This advertisement, like many others, speaks of aging as an illness, through reference to its "symptoms." The woman is a patient, who is to be treated for what is, after all, a natural process. This theme best demonstrates the underlying societal attitude toward age upon which these advertisements draw. People used to say that, if one did not like the fact of growing old, one should consider the alternative, and most would readily choose life over death. But, as Elaine Hatfield and Susan Sprecher have argued, old age all too often represents a form of social death for women; they are excluded from participation, not being found socially interesting any longer because not sexually interesting.[5] There is literally no place for them if they cannot keep up appearances.

Professional Knowledge

Besides the nurturing voice of mother and the rational, dispassionate voice of the scientist (the father substitute), a third voice assumes a more sororial tone in speaking to the consumer. Glamour magazines are filled with the faces and words of professional beauties—models and actresses— compared with whom the consumer is a rank amateur. Use of celebrities is a standard advertising technique, and one growing in popularity. Increasingly, companies are willing to pay substantial fees, part of which go to special celebrity brokers, to have celebrities tout their product and their product only.[6] Research shows that their faith is well placed, that celebrities do hold the consumer's attention and sell the product. This is especially true for adolescents.[7] The young woman seeing an endorsement from female superstars does sit up and take notice; these are women who *have* made it, they are women who are beautiful.

Such recognized beauties reflect the consumer culture's preoccupation with female beauty, with youth, and with celebrity as such. Through them, society works to reinforce conforming behavior in little girls and grown-up women. Young girls are still told "You should be an actress" or "You look just like a model." Women, then, may well assume that those others who achieve this evident pinnacle of female success, who receive society's beaming approval, must have some secret knowledge learned on the way, must have some expert tricks and craftlike skills to pass on. It is all so complicated, this beauty role. These women, at least, seem to have it under control.

Certainly some of the women featured appear ready to share secrets with the anonymous reader, almost as if she were their sister or best friend. In one, Freda Payne, television hostess of "Today's Black Woman," confesses that "people often ask me how I keep my skin so soft and young-looking. My secret? Ultra Glow Skin Tone Cream." Women are encouraged to identify with Lynda Carter as she "picks the new plums" for Maybelline (eye makeup), and to take heed when she points to her eyelid and says, "This is where a wrinkle can start." Victoria Principal tells women both how to keep fit (Jack La Lanne Health Spas) and how to have fabulous hair (Jhirmack shampoo). Advertisements provide the consumer with privileged information, such as that "Jaclyn Smith is wearing Colorfast Orchid Lights on her lips and nails," and that her eyeshadow "is a Colorfast Orchid Lights/Winter Plum duo." Even Sophia Loren appears willing to share her special fragrance with the women of the world:

> The passion of the islands
> The passion of a woman

> The passion of a fragrance
> Sophia by Coty
> Wear it with a passion

Passion is here presented as the means for achieving selfhood. It can as likely be the cause of its betrayal.

The testimonial technique, in which celebrity vouches for the superiority of the product, is a standard one in the advertising arsenal, dating from the 1920s. Lucky Strike cigarettes called upon a wide range of public figures, as did other companies, so much so that the credibility of the testimonial became undermined. As Roland Marchand writes,

> Queen Marie of Romania had given her blessing (at a price) to so many products that she became a joke in the advertising trade. Gossip about professional solicitors of endorsements, the high prices paid for testimonials, and endorsements by non-users of the product had become widespread. As early as 1926, *Printers' Ink* reported on a football player who had received $4,000 for a cigarette testimonial (presumably Lucky Strike) "notwithstanding the fact that he has never smoked and admitted that he couldn't discriminate between the aroma of a burning mattress and that of a dollar perfecto." . . . Some observers predicted that the testimonial vogue would sink beneath a tide of public ridicule after the October 29, 1927, issue of *Liberty* magazine displayed movie star Constance Talmadge's photograph and endorsement in *"eleven different advertisements of eleven different products!"*[8]

It is possible that today's advertising market may become oversaturated with professional beauties selling beauty products and disclosing beauty secrets. How, for example, are women to decide whether to follow Lynda Carter's advice on makeup colors or to adopt Jaclyn Smith's evident passion for orchid? Will

Victoria Principal help them slim, or should they remain loyal to
Jane Fonda's workout? Should they try Jane Seymour's perfume
or Sophia's?

Sometimes the celebrities get more directly involved than
simply posing for the camera and lending their name. Catherine
Deneuve has moved from supporting Chanel's perfume to
marketing her own, "Deneuve": "I've always wanted to create a
fragrance that was personal and beautiful." Model Cheryl Tiegs
now considers her line of Sears sportswear her career; she is
reported to net about $6 million a year for her efforts in design
and marketing. [9]

At times, the creative leap from product to person truly
staggers the consumer. Who would have thought to associate
New Zealand opera star Kiri Te Kanawa with Switzerland's
Rolex watches? The link made in the advertisements is her
performance and vocal staying power: how like the steady
timekeeping of the Rolex.

> "In all the years I've had the watch it's never gone off
> key and it's never been ill. And I know how hard it is to be
> 100 percent.
>
> "Every day, wherever I am, I spend at least an hour
> singing part of a role just to keep my voice at its best. So I
> can really appreciate the time, skill and effort that goes
> into something so beautiful and so precise as this watch."
>
> Kiri Te Kanawa and her Rolex Lady Datejust. No other
> voice could have put it quite so beautifully.

Advertisements starring Kiri Te Kanwa or such long-running
beauties as Joan Collins or Catherine Deneuve aim largely at
women over thirty. For younger women, fashion models become the mainstay of this genre of advertisement. Models
appear in the common imagination as unusually favored, privileged, even protected from the vicissitudes of early adulthood.

Society elevates them even as the media comments incessantly about their transition from girlhood to womanhood.

Brooke Shields became the American dreamgirl of the late 1970s and early 1980s, first fashion model, then Ivy League student, too. Advertisements encourage the fantasy that adolescent girls can become a model—"or look just like one." One popular makeup line is, in fact, named Cover Girl:

> That Cover Girl Face
> Cover Girl Kelly Emberg has it.
> The makeup for that totally natural,
> totally healthy-looking face. Your face.

As one former model has disclosed, it is often the women with the "least face" who are the most successful models. "The best models are always those with the *least* faces—i.e.—those who start with blank canvases that can be filled-in with whatever look is current."[10] Young women eagerly respond when advertisers create model searches offering a chance at beauty stardom. In one advertisement the previous winner encouraged readers thus:

> The Gentle Treatment Great Model Search Made Me a
>   Star
> Now it's your turn
> Enter the 1983 Great Model Search Today

Such model searches create great opportunities for promoting the product, the department store, and even the magazine itself. *Seventeen* magazine sponsors its own model search, with all applications processed through contest "headquarters" (namely, selected department stores) and with pages of advertisements following the contest announcement encouraging the reader to patronize the stores, buy the clothing, and enter the contest. "If you've always hoped that your fabulous face would one day gaze out from the cover of a national magazine, now's your chance to make your dream a reality."

If dream *does* become reality, the lucky winner may find that being a model is not all it is cracked up to be. In his study of high-fashion models Mark Salmon found that these models consistently downplayed the importance of their good looks. One woman emphasized instead her skill at sports, another her knowledge of foreign languages. Some pointed to intellectual achievements and interests. Salmon related these strategies of self-presentation to the fact that beauty itself is an ambiguous status.[11] We may admire beauty, but we may also distrust it. We separate it from intelligence, and only with difficulty do we reject the stereotype of the "dumb blond." Often beauty is allowed to exhibit neither character nor complexity. Anyone that attractive, we assume, must have had an easy ride.

If models and actresses are the winners in the beauty competition, the comments of certain of them should give pause for thought. A number of beauty queens have returned their coveted crowns upon finding out what was attached. Bookstores repeatedly feature the latest confession concerning some actress's rocky road not just preceding, but following, her achievement of stardom. Autobiographical and biographical accounts reveal scars on the soul not otherwise visible to the admiring public. As one example, consider the sad report on Brigitte Bardot's forty-ninth birthday:

> Her friends reserved a table for eight at Le Palmyre, a chic St. Tropez restaurant, and planned a festive celebration. . . . Hoping to cheer up the one-time sex symbol, who had been lovesick and depressed for weeks, they ordered not one but three birthday cakes—one chocolate, one lemon, one strawberry—each decorated, according to her wishes, with a single candle. But Bardot never tasted the

cakes. That afternoon, Sept. 28, while her guests sipped aperitifs at La Madrague, her beachfront St. Tropez hideaway, Bardot took a handful of sleeping pills or tranquilizers, washed them down with red wine and then, according to unconfirmed press reports, wandered out to the beach, where she was later pulled from the surf. She was rushed to the nearby L'Oasis clinic, where her stomach was pumped before she was released that evening.

"It was her birthday and she was depressed," said a lifetime confidant, and her sister explained, "Lately, she has not been in good shape. . . . I sense she is disturbed, tormented and unhappy."[12]

One could dismiss this as just so much sensationalism were it not for its embodiment of a recurrent cultural theme: the loss of self-esteem of women in general, and great beauties in particular, as they age. We repeatedly hear of Marilyn Monroes whose lives end in tragedy, the Greta Garbos who go into seclusion.

Women involved in beauty competitions, both formal and informal, of the highly televised and everyday varieties are not, however, supposed to question the goal, the overriding raison d'être that gives force and power to all this exhortation and advice, namely, great beauty, and with it, extended youth.

They also are not meant to question the source of the advice, the presumption of authority. It is not mother, but the artful representation of the mother–daughter bond by advertisers who suggest they share in its intimacy and complexity. It is not the authority of the disinterested scientist working for the benefit of humanity, but rather the scientist on the manufacturer's payroll (if not purely in the advertiser's imagination). Celebrities, as we have seen, have historically proved ready to read whatever script is handed them, if they are sufficiently rewarded for their endorsement (with, of course, the inevitable exceptions). It is one thing to envy their beauty; it is another thing to believe that it comes from a jar. But perhaps the most insidious voice is the first, the most anonymous, the one that tells us that decisions have been made by mysterious others regarding our beauty faces and fashion futures. Here, the students of the 1960s had their own piece of advice. "Question authority," they said, especially when it says its advice is disinterested, that it is given only for your own good.

FOUR
The Self Observed

Roland Barthes accurately identified one of the fundamental contradictions in the female role: namely, that a woman is supposed to make finding a man a major goal, if not *the* major goal of her life, and yet she is not supposed to act as though she is actively pursuing him.[1] If she does, she loses her innocence, her charm. She seems all too accessible, needy, and unappealing.

A woman must maintain her dignity and her mystery. She must avoid making too great a show of her ideas, interests, and emotions. Courting, the man is bold; the woman, coy. In *Hands and Hearts* historian Ellen Rothman finds such attitudes common throughout American history, constraining even the colonial maiden. "For a woman, it was not enough to be 'struck with love,' in the phrase of the day; she must await a lover. . . ."[2] Rothman finds that the Victorian lady was even more tightly bound than her predecessors by the doctrine of separate spheres and the growing restrictions on male and female interaction. As one New York schoolgirl complained of a popular work entitled *Advice to Ladies*, "It makes our intercourse with gentlemen very artificial. I cannot endure to feel restrained and guarded."[3] Even well into the twentieth century, men initiated romance and carried it through. They made the dates, conceived romantic gestures, spoke in acceptable phrases of their desires. Women assented or refused.

Although in recent decades this one-sided pattern has been slowly changing, most advertisements still conceive romance as an adventure in passivity. But, although a woman cannot openly approach the male, this does not mean that she is sitting back and doing nothing. There is instead a great deal of emotional work and beauty work going on.

To some extent, the text provided by the advertisements parallels the text Tania Modleski found in women's romance novels. Modleski believes the woman reader, who knows the romance format, knows that the strong, sullen male and the beautiful heroine will get together in the conclusion. She therefore both identifies with the heroine *and* takes the part of the hero observing her, insofar as she, the reader, knows more than the heroine. The hero–observer often catches the heroine unawares, thus having the opportunity to admire her without her knowledge and connivance. This effectively resolves Barthes' contradiction; she attracts him without willing or doing anything—unlike the sophisticated scheming woman who provides the heroine's foil and competition. The heroine retains her charm, purity, and innocence; she can do no wrong because she seems to do nothing at all.[4]

There are, however, several things she not only *can* do, but *must* do, for this happy resolution. First, she must see herself as others see her. She must take the part of the other. She must look at her mirrored reflection with the scathing eye of the born critic. As Simone de Beauvoir has written,

> For the young girl, erotic transcendence consists in becoming prey in order to gain her ends. She becomes an

object, and she sees herself as object; she discovers this
new aspect of her being with surprise: it seems to her that
she has been doubled; instead of coinciding exactly with
herself, she now begins to exist *outside.*[5]

Many advertisements address this critical eye. The woman
looks at the dress, shoes, or makeup and pictures herself
wearing them and tries to see whether or not they will *become*
her. In others, the camera appears to take the position of the
observant, but unobserved, male, hovering above her as she
sprawls across the bed, or catching an view of sexy seams as
the wind catches her skirt. Sometimes the copy reinforces the
suggestion of this unseen observer, who is also the woman
reading the advertisement. "I know. I know. You just want to
ask me a question," says the laughing Anne Klein model in her
fashionable gear, sitting on the floor and clearly amused by
whatever it is we might want to ask. The Caress soap model
turns her head to look at us, as we admire the lovely expanse of
her smooth back, "You dress to look breathtaking. You caress
to feel soft." Like the implicit male, we can almost reach out and
touch her velvet skin. As Walter Benjamin has suggested,
looking through the camera has become an accepted, if not the
dominant, way of perceiving "reality."[6] The ideal is to make
one's appearance unforgettable, so that one's actions become
redundant. The product is part of the process, even if it is only
one's choice in cigarettes:

> Once seen, never forgotten
> That's me. And my More.
> My More is richer. Longer.
> More tasteful.
> Anyone can spot that.

The leggy blond poses in swimsuit, staring straight at the
camera, challenging it (him) to gainsay her claim. In another in

the series, an attractive black woman in evening dress leans back against a grand piano, her long lean cigarette part of the essential *équipage:* "Something special. That's me and my More . . . It's all there for you to see."

It is no wonder, then, that the mirror is the symbol of femininity. It is not vanity; it is necessity. It reflects the commandment that women see themselves as others see them; it is the means by which they can be at once both self (critic) and other (object). If the critic disapproves of the object, if nothing she puts on *becomes* her, then it is time for more drastic action, a complete overhaul, in short, a makeover.

The idea of the beauty makeover promises the woman that by bestowing one's faith in makeup artists, hair stylists, and fashion experts, and by spending money on new makeup, hairdo, and wardrobe, she can discard the ugly old self and step into a beautiful new self, achieving what society told her all along was her natural birthright.

> From Unnoticed
> Donna and Kara, before
> To Unforgettable.
> The Beautiful, believable transformation:
> A Portrait of Possibilities for You.

> Seeing is believing say the mother and daughter pictured here . . . "A realistic change for the better. The opportunity to rethink ourselves within the context of our own lives and emerge with a renewed and glowing sense of self." "Look at Mom. Isn't she beautiful!" daughter Kara exclaims. The pictures tell the tale.

When a woman rethinks her self, here it is defined as her beauty self. A realistic change is a beauty change. The content of her life derives from her appearance; changing the latter is sure to change the former. Other makeover advertisements put the point even more bluntly. In a two-page advertisement contrasting the before and after of makeover iconography, Regis hair stylists encourage the consumer, "Change your life—permanently."

Makeover stories in advertisements are echoed by the editorial content, most particularly in magazines aimed at women who want to lose weight. Self-approval is low among overweight women, who often reflect in their own opinion society's low appraisal of their femininity, of their sexuality. They often dream of how losing weight, combined with a new hairdo and makeup, might indeed change their life "permanently." Among the many women featured in one leading weight-loss magazine was thirty-eight-year-old Frances, who "came to the studio admitting she felt badly in need of a new look." Linda also vowed, "I really need help in every direction. . . . My hair's in bad condition and my makeup needs updating." To their rescue come the beauty experts, eager fairy godmothers able to transform poor Cinderella into the belle of the ball. Through their wizardry, Frances gets a fancy face and new haircut, she feels "years better, younger." Linda too feels fantastic: "My new hairstyle couldn't be easier to manage—and I promise to practice my new make-up . . . Thanks for giving me my confidence back!"

Sometimes such makeovers do "make over" the outside mien of a woman. That so much faith is placed in them reflects how much importance is placed on the external appearance of women, and how little concern is given to what goes on inside them. Little concern has been expressed, at least since Henry Higgins' exasperated appeal that women make over their minds, to "making over" attitudes, politics, mentality, intellect. By feminists, yes, but by them alone.

In fairy tales, all romances end happily. In reality, it is often a different story. English writer Jill Tweedie has chronicled the crimes and misdemeanors that have been committed *In the Name of Love*. The earliest meaning of *romance* was "adventure," but this was implicitly a male adventure. As Tweedie points out, chivalry itself may be seen as the greatest excuse men ever invented for leaving the company of women.[7] Such attitudes and legitimation reoccur throughout Western history, from the *Roman de la Rose* to the Cavalier poet's concluding lines, "I could not love thee, dear, so much,/Loved I not honor more." Today, honor may be less valued, but women are still prized as trophies in this form of manly competition.

Getting His Attention, Guessing His Wishes, Obeying His Commands

Having passed her own critical evaluation, the woman is now ready to meet the male. Independent action is still largely proscribed. Instead, she relies on her appearance *to speak for her*. The well-developed identity of the products help fill out the underdeveloped identity of the woman, while protecting her from social blunders. Verbal interaction becomes irrelevant, when Joyce shoes proclaim, "I'm Joyce, Who are you?" The copy reinforces the point: "Wear Joyce this Spring and announce yourself. You won't be forgotten." Clothes, makeup, and accessories become not simply one form of communication, but rather the *only* form of communication necessary. The first impression becomes the only impression, thus reinforcing the stereotype that the only important identity for a woman is her visible identity, her beauty identity.

Thus appearance becomes identity and woman's main line of action. In acting out her beauty role, the woman needs men as props and backdrop. Mysterious hands come out to embrace lovable faces or to light cigarettes; the reader is free to imagine the face of the attached male, to complete the text herself. In the Nivea advertisement, a male hand caresses the exposed back of a woman in smoky blue fur: "Nivea. For over seventy years, it's been appreciated by more women and men than any other moisturizer." Male heads are there to lean on, and to appreciate the softness of a hairdo: "Feel the difference . . . Enriched with precious mink oil, for a soft, silky, touchable hold." Male models are shown as escorts (Carefree panty liners), supports (the comfortably clad model in the Tultex sweats advertisement finds a man she can lean on), and audiences ("I find myself more and more beautiful . . ." says the svelte Rodier model, using the opportunity provided by workmen carrying a piece of reflective glass to reapply lipstick. They join in admiring her mirrored reflection). Men are also necessary as the second half of that hallowed institution, the couple, walking under the trees, sailing into sunsets (Merit cigarettes), or drinking cognac ("Martell Cordon Bleu, of course").

To transform audience into actor, prop into proposition, the woman must not simply get his attention. She must also guess his wishes and obey his commandments. How can she attract the "right" man? Tania Modleski provides the answer: she must *read* him like a text.[8]

The young blond in lace and denim speaks through the soft-focus mist of devotion: "Without telling me, he told me. He loves the way I look, when I look this way." Just as in the romance novels, men in advertisements are initially unwilling to speak their heart. Women have to guess; they have to read the signs. Sometimes, though, men provide a clue:

He says he loves me for my sense of humor. Ha.

He laughed when I said I always have a hot dog before the ballet.

But then, it's easy to get a laugh when you're playing to a captive audience.

Frankly, I think he's pretty special, too. So tonight, I wanted to look nothing less than sensational. And I wasn't about to trust my hair to anything less than Finesse . . .

Sure, he thinks I'm funny. But the way he looks at me (when we're not laughing) says he's noticing more than just my wit.

While women are constrained in how openly they can seduce the male, they are allowed whatever acts of deception will help them in that effort. Here we see a critical difference between romance novels and female advertisements. Unlike the classic virginal heroine, we are not all innocent and pure, and we are not all born beautiful. Some part of us must play the role of the scheming little adventuress. We must rely on artifice; we must learn to deceive. Deception itself is presented as an archetypal female act, and beauty secrets are accepted weapons in the female arsenal. A man may well suspect some secrets—that a woman dyes her hair, or wears false eyelashes. But that's not the half of it. As the chic model receives admiring glances, she confides to the reader, "Nobody knows I'm wearing support pantyhose."

Because Hanes Alive gives me all the support I need, but doesn't give me away. Alive is so beautifully sheer . . . nobody will ever know my secret.

Barielle discovered the secret to longer, stronger nails. Massage his ego. Take up the piano. Or even touch football. Now your nails can survive it all.

In this last advertisement, it's clear that achieving appearances, whether of long nails or a passion for football, is more important than any identity or interests the woman has achieved out of her own drives or for her own amusement.

From reading the advertisements, one might conclude that there were a large number of leg men out there. Women are repeatedly told that "Gentlemen prefer Hanes," with the model in short skirts getting all the attention. L'eggs pantyhose also asserts that "Ladies with L'eggs Have Choices" and promises, "The more you choose L'eggs, the more you get chosen." Hanes employs the narrative technique in having a male rhapsodize about his beloved's outstanding qualities:

REFLECTIONS ON MELISSA

She taught me how to tie a perfect bow tie.
Say "I love you" in seventeen languages.
And her legs . . . Melissa's incredible legs.

That's Melissa. Julie "has an absolute passion for Billie Holiday" and "sees nothing in Picasso." As for Joanna, she "messes up the punchline of every joke," but "can tell a Burgundy from a Bordeaux. And her legs . . . oh yes, Joanna's legs."

Julie, Joanna, and Melissa are all good companions. They'd be nice to go to dinner with—savvy, flirtatious, feminine, and not too challenging. But above all else, it is their legs that their men find most attractive. By contrast, advertisements do not seem to exploit the preferences of breast men. We don't, for example, hear one sighing, "And her tits . . . oh yes, Alison's tits."

When the male concerned is a husband, his tastes become commandments. Oil of Olay relies upon the testimonial technique by photographing a beautiful Italian woman who shares her beauty secret as she leans invitingly from her balcony:

When my husband comes home at night, he wants to see a nice, pretty face . . . my face.
I met my husband when he was studying medicine in Italy and we were married there almost 4 years ago . . .

He still thinks I'm very pretty and I want him to believe that . . .

I have my little tricks. Part of my day is Oil of Olay Beauty Fluid . . . I put on Oil of Olay every night after I wash my face. My husband doesn't like greasy creams so this is good.

Here this husband's pleasures are interpreted as dictates. The advertisement also reinforces the emphasis on marriage to a doctor as one of the payoffs for female beauty, but beauty that must be maintained if the marriage is to last.

If one does not have a man on hand to *read* as a text, the second-best thing is to read what other men are willing to say about their tastes, hoping again to pick up significant clues and guidelines. When Oscar de la Renta insists, "I know what makes a woman beautiful," women are supposed to listen. When Bill Blass lists "What I like and don't like so much in a woman," women are supposed to take note. For the record, his dislikes are

1. A woman who talks about dieting all the time
2. Who does crossword puzzles in ink
3. A woman who jogs and tells
4. A woman whose perfume is too loud for her looks
5. A woman who can't pass a mirror without looking into it
6. A woman who won't gossip
7. Who worries about getting her hair wet in the rain
8. Who won't admit she reads cheap novels
9. Who wouldn't spend her last few bucks on perfume.

By contrast, his likes are listed as

1. A woman who seems to be listening, even if she isn't
2. A woman who loves a good laugh

3. Who can get gorgeously dressed in 15 minutes flat
4. Who can cuss in five languages
5. Who prefers almost anything to white wine
6. Who's a great dancer
7. Who's a big eater
8. A woman who doesn't cry at weddings
9. Loves clothes, but doesn't talk about them
10. Who would spend her last few bucks on perfume. Hopefully mine.

To recapitulate, an *unattractive* woman for Blass is one smart enough to answer the crossword without hesitation, disciplined enough to jog and diet, and with sufficient personal honor *not* to talk about her friends behind their backs. She is concerned about her appearance, as Blass might hope all women to be, but she makes the grave error of letting that concern show to men. She thus violates the earlier stated expectation that a woman can be charming or beautiful only when she appears unconscious of her appeal, this though her very appeal is created only through her continued awareness of and attention to it. This woman is unattractive, in short, because she is boring to men.

The *attractive* woman, by contrast, is above all amusing. She looks gorgeous but, unlike the unattractive woman, she does not have to work at it. Blass, creator of high-priced artifice, here demands a natural beauty. She can get stunningly dressed in no time at all, eat all she wants and still be trim, loves clothes and perfume, but knows not to bore her mate by talking about such feminine topics. Instead, she "loves a good laugh" (at his jokes), seems to be listening (to him, of course), and prefers almost anything to white wine (shares his tastes).

The Power of a Woman

There is a reward for all this attention to appearance and detail. As Modleski writes regarding romance novels, their endings reverse the dominant order as the hero is overpowered by the woman, by her love, virtue, and beauty. Such is also true in the text of these advertisements, where the use of beauty products gives women sexual power over men.[9]

Sometimes this power is exhibited in what Baudrillard called *le défi*,[10] the defiant gesture in seduction. Sexuality is not rational; it is disruptive. As Freud told us, civilization and sexuality exist at odds; the former has to tame the latter. Sexual drives must be subliminated into other channels of expression: into work, into art, into religion.[11] Not so in the advertisements, however, where women's special knack at disrupting the best-laid plans of men through powerful potions and outrageous fashions is openly celebrated. In the advertisement for a Coty fragrance, the copy reads "Disturb the peace:" A brunette in the red leotard looks surprised as the squadron of muscle men fight it out all around her. "We mixed the essence of Patchouli and WILD MUSK and got something explosively different." In another advertisement a sad-faced fellow named Brian begs

> Ladies.
> My name is Brian.
> And I'm asking you to stop wearing all this wild Natural Wonder makeup. It's like—color out of control. The simple fact is—I can't take it. Call me weak, I'll admit it. But when I see a girl in that "tiger eye" lipstick with that "hot shot red" eyeshadow, I just—well I kinda make a fool of myself. I know the makeup is good for your skin . . . But a guy can only take so many gorgeously colored lips and eyes and cheeks and nails before *something* happens. Think about it.

That something, presumably, is a sexual response, a surrender to the power of female appearance. We find its presumed aftermath in the Revlon advertisement with its Chinoiserie overtones (exotic jewelry, Chinese teapot, and silks). The narrow-eyed model is pressed up against the wall. "It was only after he left that she came to her senses."

> She blamed it on The Tea Silks.
> Revlon's luxurious and tawny hues for Spring.

Perhaps because their product is invisible, because they cannot rely upon transmitting information about smell through print, perfume manufacturers often favor advertisements in which "something happens." That something is often the surrender of male to female, as in "Your Wind Song stays on his mind," or "Tigress . . . The fragrance so feline and female, it makes grown men purr." But perfumes do not just help initiate sex; more remarkable, they inspire love:

> Tatiana . . . for a woman to love and a man to remember.

> Ruffles, a fragrance to love and be loved in.

> Live like you're in love . . . and you will be.

All is fair in love and war. In the terms of beauty advertising, this translates into the advantage gained by the woman who buys the product before her competitor does. Maybe money does not buy everything, but in these advertisements it does buy you love—and all the material goods that are supposed to come with it.

KISS HIM GOODBYE, MAGGIE

It was easy . . . taking him away from you was a breeze. I deserve him. I have the best things in life; cars, boats and now *him*.

He's so HOT. But he'll have to cool off . . . for now. Go find yourself another guy, Maggie, he's *mine* now.

It is not the woman who is property in this advertisement, but the man: the role reversal that Modleski so well describes. He may be sexually steamy, but he will have to cool off. She gives the orders, she maintains control.

The woman gets what she wants, whether it is love, sex, or expensive vacations. In the February 1987 *Vogue* advertisement for Gucci, a conversation is taking place in an expensive apartment. "How about Capri," he asks. "I guess May is good," says the well-dressed woman, half-lit by the French windows. "Not too many tourists." "Capri is good anytime," he responds. She gives her command: "O.K., then, book us at the Quisiana." But the next month, on holiday, she is bored. In this second advertisement she stands dejected in white knit up against a palm. "Is everything OK?" the absent male asks in the copy. "Everything's fine . . . . It's just, I want to go back." As with most open-ended texts, as with soap opera serials aimed at women, this Gucci narrative may be continued.

Advertisements such as these encourage women to see themselves as others, men in particular, see them. But it is more complicated than this, for advertisements sell products that various individual men may like, dislike, or simply ignore. It *may* be the stockings. Or it may be the legs. It may be the dress or it may be the body. "It" may even be something quite different, unique to the woman, something that cannot be bottled, packaged, or sold.

As much as advertisements pretend to rejoice in the unique "you," they sell to the "us," the mass of consumers. When we see ourselves as others see us, our reflection is a complicated layering of social ideas and images and our impressions of them. Unlike the romantic heroine, the modern woman can ill afford to maintain an innocent eye, not when it comes to the demanding business of putting on appearances.

FIVE

Sex and Romance

It would be wrong to read these advertisements simply as an adventure in passivity. As suggested in the preceding chapter, many of these static images have a narrative feel to them. In their own way they offer what Roland Barthes has defined as the "pleasure of the text." They evoke images and inspire the imagination of consumers. As with the psychologists' TAT tests, where intriguing pictures are used as the basis of subjects' stories, here the advertisement inspires the woman to dream her own story. Paralleling Barthes' discussion, there are two forms this story making can take.

The first has a closed-ended format with a familiar ending—"And they lived happily ever after." This is the land of fairy tales; this is the magical world of romance. The heroines are young, innocent, fair, and pure. They rise with their lover to a higher state, presumably holy matrimony. If Barthes is right, these images create a sense of *plaisir,* pleasure or satisfaction in happy and orderly outcomes.

But another form of transcendence, or at least escape from

the everyday, is provided by tales in which the woman does not rise to a higher, more sacred, status, but rather descends into the dark, the sensual, the faintly sinister. The heroine of these narratives is not the fair maiden but the dark lady, these two comprising the dominant stereotypes of Western womanhood. The dark lady is erotic and exotic. She, and the consumer reading the advertisement, experience not *plaisir* but *jouissance*, a sensual delight not at achieving order but at exploding into erotic disorder, of passionate release.[1] Let us see, now, how these two narratives and these two stereotypes appear in the advertisements.

The Fair Maiden

Women traditionally were—and, if we go by the advertisements, still are—defined by their sexual availability. The fair maiden doesn't; the dark lady does. In the first stereotype, be she virgin or mother, the women is taken as innocent. Her sexuality is either unstated or understated. In the advertisements, soft-focus photography reveals the model in a narcissistic, self-involved pose, perhaps gazing at her own reflection in a pond or contemplating the petals on a flower. She is surrounded by greenery, by whispery willows: alone in nature save, perhaps, a favored pet (the male substitute). The viewer is implied but seldom seen; as suggested in the previous chapter, she must remain innocent of his intruding gaze.

   In many perfume advertisements the virgin, or fair maiden, is equated with a flower. She is the "Fleurs de Fleurs" of Nina Ricci. She wears "Ombre Rose," the "one fragrance that will make you forget all others" (as he will forget all other women). She knows how to "steal a little thunder from a rose" with Tea Rose. Sometimes, her beauty is not limited to a single blossom but, rather, is likened unto a garden:

Only Oscar de la Renta could capture the memory of a dawn lit garden. Enter the garden. Envelop yourself in the luxury and elegance of Oscar de la Renta.

> They say romance is back in style
> I say it never went out
> Le Jardin de Max Factor
> The incurably romantic fragrance.

Victorian art and social critic John Ruskin was sharing in the wisdom of his day when he described woman as a delicate blossom. Too much waving in the wind, too much activity, was sure to destroy her beauty.[2] In the advertisements, what is communicated is the sense that any rude contact with reality might spoil the maiden's perfection. And so she retreats into the soft-focus dream world of Anäis Anäis, wherein the dressing-table mirror reflects soft feminine faces, orchids, and pearls. Or she takes herself off to the poppy fields of Jontue, in which a young woman lies across the back of a large white horse. She (not the horse) is "sensual—not too far from innocence."

But there is more to being a flower than being delicate. Georges Bataille points out that the whole colorful show of petals and fragrance is there simply to attract fertilization, nothing more. That is, after all, the point.[3] Like the flower, women should be soft, fragrant, moist, and inviting: "Moisture. It gives life to a flower. MoistureWear Make-up. It gives life to the look and feel of your skin." Skin, nails, lips, and, presumably, genitals, should all be wet: "Which nail is the wet one?" . . . "Does your skin feel like it's dying of thirst?" . . . "What lips thirst for." A beautiful white swan splashes through the crystalline blue water: "Vanderbilt. Let it release the splendor of you." When a woman is dried up, she is without splendor. She is out of the sexual competition.

Not surprisingly, given the premium placed on freshness,

many advertisements emphasize youth and innocence. "I feel very Chantilly today," says the blond ingenue surrounded by lace in a long-running advertisement. She symbolizes youth and beauty; her feelings presumably have the authority granted to virgins in more traditional societies. She is half-child and half-woman, posed perilously between the two ages and with a liminal power all her own. In another advertisement she is in the role of teenage sweetheart, shyly sharing a couch with her boyfriend:

> Some of the nicest things happen in Love's Baby Soft.
> The soft, tender, totally feminine fragrance.
> It's like a smile
> from deep inside.

Such seemingly attractive and popular girls present role models for magazine readers. Theirs is a winning image of what adolescent girls should strive for: femininity, beauty, popularity. *Seventeen* magazine describes itself as "Where the girl ends and the woman begins." Advertisers are invited to participate in modeling this Galatea.

Advertisements communicate clearly that only the most feminine girls attract the best-looking boys. No question is raised as to whether boys and men actually *like* women who consider themselves "incurable romantics." Rather, they are presented as being willing co-conspirators: of desiring romantic love as avidly as women do. The dreamy couple in ruffled riding gear have dismounted by a sunlit riverbank. The copy reads, "If you believe in one great love as many people do . . . then you should wear Jontue. Wear it and be wonderful."

Romantic fragrances are associated with beginnings: "Chanel No. 22 The Beginning." They depict first encounters and first loves. Although youth is important, the truly feminine woman may remain a romantic in her heart however far she stands from that first blush of innocence:

She always cries at weddings? Your tender-hearted mother will treasure the romantic scent, L'Air du Temps . . . the fragrance for young lovers. And that, of course, means all lovers, because warm hearts *never grow old.*

With the right beauty products, the woman can always have the sense of newness, of freshness. "A new way of looking / a new way of feeling / A new L'Oréal to warm the cockles of your heart." The accompanying photograph shows a wayward romantic, a fashionably dressed vagabond, without a care in her head. There is no pretense of sophistication: these are wholesome girls given to wearing "homespun colors" in lipsticks and "kissing cousins" lip gloss.

True romantics approach the changing of the seasons with a similar innocence. They "awaken to a new spring" with Lancôme or to a "Straw Hat Spring with" L'Oréal.

> A new freshness
> A new clearness
> A new L'Oréal to stir the soul
> Candy Apple lips, Rose Bouquet fingertips
> Bleu Antique / Pink Voile eyes.

Fair maidens are encouraged to rejoice in country summers and the colors of autumn. They dream of wintry evenings without reflecting on more somber connotations—relying, presumably, on the L'Air du Temps assurance that warm hearts never grow old.

Much of the female socialization encourages this romantic rendering of sexual desire. The girl herself is meant to live as in a fairy-tale stupor. She waits to be awakened—sexually, emotionally, even intellectually—by her prince ("Especially feminine nightwear . . . from a line of sleeping beauties from J. C. Penney"). When this happens, she quickly signs the marriage contract and visits the bridal registry, because, as Oneida silver knows, "Love lasts," and, as the china manufacturer tells her in the pages of *Seventeen,* "Love leads to Lenox."

The Dark Lady

"Part of the art of being a woman," advises actress Jaclyn Smith, "is knowing when not to be too much of a lady." If the virgin or fair maiden represents one polar type of feminine sexuality, at the other extreme sits the dark lady, the woman of mystery, oftimes in folklore and literature—the whore. On one side is innocence and romance; on the other, knowledge and sexuality.

Jaclyn Smith favors "Epris . . . a most provocative fragrance" for those times when she decides to act less than ladylike. In another advertisement a woman is posed dramatically in black evening gown and red face mask before a half-open mahogany door, the other side of which, presumably, a man sits waiting. Like Smith, the model knows how to "seize the moment" by wearing Scoundrel, "a brave a beautiful new spirit in fragrance." Things have progressed further in the Masquerade "Unleash Your Fantasies" advertisement, where the masked male partygoer is unzipping his sequined female counterpart, embracing him in passionate ecstasy. None of the other guests notices.

Some advertisements treat sexuality as a bright and happy plaything. Charlie is "the gorgeous, sexy-young fragrance." In others, the copywriters display a heavier, more sensual touch. Charles Beau offers up "Le Parfum:"

> An intrusion. Subtle
> Sensuous
> Surrender to Charles Beau

The accompanying photograph depicts a woman prone on the floor, one arm thrown over her head, the other at her breast. A man's shadow looms over her. In the controversial Calvin Klein advertisements for Obsession, no copy is necessary. All we need see is the smoky, confused image of what appears to be a threesome. This is the sexual disorder of *jouissance*.

Much of the erotic kick comes from the breaking of social boundaries, real or pretended. Eroticism occurs at the *edges*— the physical edges of body and material (edges of lace, fashion cut-outs)—and the edges of society, its back streets and dark corners.[4]

Advertisements play with the edges and boundaries of society, of right and proper female behavior. Increasingly, they must pretend that the norm still exists, in order to give women the pleasure of breaking it. The female body, alluringly decorated, is disruptive. Lawman denim fashions tell women, simply, "Break the Law." Maybelline lipstick promises a "shine this outrageous" ("Set a shining example. Show them what lip color was meant to be. Devastating . . . Leaps and bounds beyond the ordinary").

Sexuality is a form of transgression. The long-running Tabu advertisement showed a violinist overcome by his accompanist's perfume, breaking the taboo against romantic involvement. "Poison is my potion" says the dark lady with the long sinuous black lace glove (exactly what Barthes was describing), and the copy confirms that Poison perfume is "the newest enchantress." Opium is "for those who are addicted to Yves Saint Laurent."

The new perfumes suggest the New Decadence; one is even named Decadence. The first page in a two-page advertisement is a black-and-white photograph by Helmet Newton labeled *"L'Ultime Séduction,"* Paris, 1985. A man in black tie is kissing a woman in sequined evening dress with a long leg slit, both are perilously leaning against the art nouveau railing of a spiral staircase. In the second photograph (*"La Séduction du Bain,"* New York, 1987), the man in black tie is reflected in the woman's elegant mirror. With her silk embroidered robe falling off one shoulder, she, however, is looking away, more captivated by the jar of body lotion she holds in her hand. In each advertisement, the product is presented in color, with art nouveau framing, while the rest is black and white. Both the perfume featured in the first advertisement and the bath products ("Body Decadence") in the second advertisement are described as "Opulent. Uninhibited luxury." Great sex, the suggestion is, takes considerable wealth.

The amoral rich, real or fictional, are held up as examples for commoners to enjoy, perhaps to emulate. In recent years their paragons were the threesome collectively known as "The Diors." They were introduced as follows:

> Meet the Diors: The Wizard, the Mouth, and Oliver. When they were good they were very, very good and when they were bad they were gorgeous.

Magazine readers were provided with their early history:

> When the Mouth was a little girl she had asthma. She had to stay in bed and smoke long, black asthma cigarettes that the Wizard gave her. Oliver would come home after school to watch.

They were given the Diors' predilections:

> The Diors heard no evil and saw no evil, but nothing could stop the Mouth.

> They loved armadillos, the American flag and they disliked all their friends equally.

Finally, the Diors married:

> The Diors took the oath to have and to hold, for better or
> worse. Forsaking all others, they vowed: "I do." "I do."
> "And I do, too."

The playful immorality suggested by the idea of the threesome,
the older and younger man (as attracted to each other as to the
woman) and Oliver's perchant for watching might amuse some
women. But Women Against Pornography (WAP) were not
among them. Noting in particular two advertisements in the
series that showed the two men (both named and fully clothed)
ganging up on the woman (identified by a physical trait, "The
Mouth," and half-exposed), WAP representative Dorchen
Leidholdt said, "These ads trivialize women, celebrate a power
imbalance between men and women, and make sexual games
with sadomasochistic overtones seem chic and glamourous."
The managing director of the advertising firm responded, "Dior
is satisfied with the sales response, the positive attitude
shifts—and with Richard Avedon" (the prestigious photograph-
er). Dior may have been satisfied, but one certified Beautiful
Person, Jacqueline Onassis, was not. When a Jackie O look-alike
appeared in one of the advertisements, the real one sued.

In these and similar advertisements the woman is encouraged to imagine herself in the role of the sophisticate, the
"élégante." Her knowledge can take one of two forms: either
the mastery of the social forms of postindustrial urban culture or
of the mysterious mores of presumably preindustrial foreign
cultures: the exotic East, Near East, India, and Africa. Both
draw upon the stereotype of the *femme fatale*. An advertisement
for Halston fragrance shows a recumbent woman holding her
moisturizer, with a sculpture of a pawing jaguar in the background. The suggestion is that the woman using Halston will,
like the jaguar, be mysterious, feline, dangerous. A second

designer fragrance, Norell, relies on a dramatic photograph of the Manhattan skyline to impress consumers with its sophisticated image. Opium, clearly designed to be one of the exotic fragrances, heralded the introduction of its line of bath products as follows:

> From Paris comes an opulent new bath regimen—a sequence of exotic fragrances . . . As you open the richly lacquered red and magenta boxes with golden accents, you'll be entranced by the heady combination of spices, woods, fruits, and the warm notes such as myrrh.

Exotic settings promise sensual delights forbidden in mainstream Western society. This sensuality derives from images of warm sand, of wild animals (and men), of unfamiliar mores, including sexual mores. Elizabeth Arden "Primitives" conjure up "savage sands, wild fires . . . primitive corals for your lips, nails, cheeks, eyes." Ultima II features Safari colors (with shades of Flamingo, Endangered Blue, Silvered Ivory) and promises that "any place you wear the glamour new Safari collection—backyard, out to dinner, your job—will be a wilder place than before you showed up." Finally, a black model wearing "African Wild Colors" invites the consumer to "explore the daring of Jungle Fuchsia . . . the depth of African Coral . . . the gleam of Tropic Bronze."

Many of these more openly seductive advertisements rely on brutality chic to sell their products, Shoes in particular call up the sexual aggression between women and men. Women's shoes are presented as weapons used both by and against them. The tortuous high heel thus becomes an object of brutality in a sadomasochistic game that can be played both ways. An advertisement for men's boots advises, "Treat 'em good and they'll treat you good," and shows a woman pulling off a man's black cowboy boots. "In the Old West, it's said, some men took better care of their boots than their women. Not altogether admirable, but certainly understandable."

In such advertisements sadism becomes understandable, and aggression is presented as a daily part, even a desirable part, of daily life. Rayne shoes depicts two exotic beauties pulling each other's hair. They're competing for the red and white sandals, "worth fighting for." Interestingly, brutality chic appears in its strongest form in advertisements for the most expensive shoes. Charles Jourdan features a $420 yellow stiletto boot in a broken window pane surrounded by more broken glass, a woman's hand appears clutching a brown object—or weapon. A less expensive brand, Jem's also wants to be "for the daring," encouraging women to "look like you spend recklessly." What matters is the fantasy, not the reality, of a "walk on the wild side."

Part of the sexual thrill is the rapid assuming of identities. This is particularly seen in makeup advertisements, wherein women are encouraged to create "Allures" with Elizabeth Arden's "high impact lips" and to achieve sex appeal through "Flex Appeal . . . the Adjustable Angle Mascara. . . ." Even the respectable old house of Chanel encourages a certain sexual excitement with "Rouge Extreme. Daring new high-intensity lip color. Concentrated to make a lasting impression." The contrast is clearly between the rapid application of makeup, its relative transience, and the permanent impression it must etch in the hearts of men.

> Do it!
> Have you ever wanted to
> . . . but didn't?
> Have you ever been asked
> . . . but wouldn't?
> Should you or shouldn't you?
> Why not give in and DO IT?
> DO IT for you . . . DO IT for him.

And when you "DO IT," do it with
La Maur Natural Woman "DO IT" cosmetic collections.

In all such advertisements a process of seduction takes place
on two separate levels. The woman seduces the man, but it is
also true that the manufacturer seduces the woman. Key
phrases include "You won't be able to resist," and, of course,
"Enjoy." A woman should not simply give in to temptation; she
should revel in it:

TEMPTATIONS
for springtime lips, nails, cheeks, eyes
THE FLIRTATIOUS FUCHSIAS
THE IRRESISTIBLE REDS
THE CAPTIVATING CORALS
All the color temptations you won't be able to resist.

There is, however, a problem. Heavy makeups and provocative perfumes have the disadvantage of appearing indiscrimi-
nate; all men stand to get the message. The problems this poses
for everyday life should be obvious. Lingerie, on the other hand,
has the advantage of being aimed (at least in theory) at a more
selected audience. By implication, it can be more openly
seductive and arousing. "First the Vassarette. What goes on
after that is up to you."

As the Lily of France name suggests, sexy lingerie is
associated with France, more specifically, with images of the
French bordello, the tension between the licit and illicit, the
cultural play of fashion itself:

The new French Connection. Once you've worn it you can
never plead innocent. Experience the French Connection
and you'll discover the secret pleasures of French-inspired
lingerie. Bras that are little more than a bare hug of

shimmering color. Panties cut higher on the thigh, so you look leggier. Shimmering nylon in a line-up of arresting colors from Lily of France.

Such advertisements encourage women to discard their social roles in a form of libidinal retreat. They encourage a layering of identities: serious on the outside, sensual on the inside. In that most curious and classic of lingerie advertisements, the Maidenform woman appeared in bra and underpants, looking serious as she went about her business in bank vault, concert hall, or even medical ward. While she took her place in a man's world, underneath she was reassuringly all woman. The man, or men, always operated oblivious to this half-clad woman. They served as mere scenery and backdrop. She alone commanded center stage, oblivious to them, sufficient audience unto herself.

This and other advertisements reinforce the image of female sexuality as narcissistic. It is her own body that the woman finds appealing and that provides her greatest turn-on. "It's hard to believe that anything this tiny and shiny and sassy and sexy could hold you and mold you and shape you and make you more beautiful than any bra you've ever worn."

The long-running Maidenform campaign had been targeted by feminists, who rightly interpreted it as trivializing women's efforts to achieve equal standing. (The female doctor in the bright red underwear was the last straw.) In their effort to change gender assumptions, they were following the lead of their late eighteenth-century foremother Mary Wollstonecraft. In *A Vindication of the Rights of Woman,* Wollstonecraft argued that the choice offered women then, as now, romance and sensuality, was no choice at all. Both romance *and* sensuality represented for Wollstonecraft forms of irrationality. What she advocated instead was an emphasis on reason, to be fully accepted as rational beings rather than unstable emotional creatures.[5] In most advertisements, reason is downplayed. The choice is not among products but among images, hence, all the soft-focus, visually stunning, happy days and sexy nights.

Certain products, however, *do* ask women to apply the light of reason to their sexual escapades. These advertisements are relatively new, as is their frankness:

> "I never thought I'd buy a condom," says the attractive model, looking the reader in the eye.
>
> "Let's face it, sex these days can be risky business, and you need all the protection you can get. Between the fear of unplanned pregnancy, sexually transmitted diseases, and the potential side effects of many female contraceptives, it may seem like sex is hardly worth the risk anymore."

This is, as Mentor contraceptives describes it, "smart sex in the '80's." A change of pace and of tack from the romantic prelude. A second condom advertisement puts the issues even more bluntly:

> "I enjoy sex, but I'm not ready to die for it"
>
> "I never thought having an intimate relationship with someone could be a matter of life or death. But with everything I hear about AIDS these days, I'm more than uncomfortable. I'm afraid."
>
> AIDS isn't just a gay disease, it's everybody's disease.
> And everybody who gets it dies.

This is the new realism. It was all very well to say love hurts. But sexually transmitted diseases kill.

Will women be able quickly to switch modes, from being romantically innocent, to seductively available, to being practical and self-protective? Some shy away from these complexities and contradictions, as sexual abstinence becomes part of the New Sobriety ("Just Say No").[6] For others, the sexual narrative is essential the same old story, but with new obstacles to be overcome. In a social world where the old gender norms have broken down, the play itself becomes the thing. As men and women perform their own versions, the difficulty lies in finding a desirable other who is willing to read from a matching sexual script.[7] Magazine advertisements provide plot possibilities; what goes on after that, as one advertisement says, is up to you.

SIX

Beauty Status /
Social Status

For women, beauty has traditionally been one route to achieving social status. By "marrying up," the beauty can wave good-bye to her humble origins and gain recognition, and security, among her "betters." This once achieved, she then needs to reflect the social status of her husband. Through the purchase and use of expensive luxury goods, including fashion and beauty products, she communicates to one and all his wealth and earning power. She becomes a luxury object herself as through her shopping, fashion display, and evident leisure she performs what Thorstein Veblen called "vicarious consumption" for her husband.[1] It is obvious: he must be rich and/or powerful if he can afford *her.*

Status goods are essential signs in a mobile society where people do not have a long-running knowledge of each other and each other's family inheritance or social position. We communicate quickly where we stand in social status.[2] One of the most easily read signs of status is our appearance: our posture, our clothing, our overall presentation of self.

Advertisements promise that products can be read by others; the advertisements themselves help create shared meanings as to what goods have high status, based in large measure on how much they cost. Money is the common standard by which products of great range and variety can all be judged; what is worth more, a diamond ring or a fur coat? Well, how much did it *cost?* What is truly unique or distinctive about the product fades as this one standard is imposed. The value we place on the product is as real to us—even more so—than any specific character or quality of the product, which may be less easily communicated, less commonly shared. This necklace may come from my mother, but you don't know that; you, in short, cannot see how much it is *worth.*[3]

Given the importance of this one standard, this monetary standard for judging relative worth, many advertisements forego description of the product's contents or presumed appeal, stressing instead only its exorbitant price. High cost has one particular desired effect: it is meant to inspire envy in others, to insure that the status position of the wearer is recognized by one and all. This ability to inspire envy is, for social critic John Berger, the very definition of glamour: "Publicity is about social relations, not objects. Its promise is not of pleasure, but of happiness: happiness as judged from the outside by others. The happiness of being envied is glamour."[4] This happiness of being envied provides "a solitary form of reassurance." Others look at you with interest; you do not respond. If you do, says Berger, "you will become less enviable. . . . It is this which explains the absent, unfocused look of so many glamour images. They look out *over* the looks of envy which sustains them."[5]

As stated earlier, a man's appearance communicates his *power* to affect others. A woman's appearance, by contrast, communicates her *presence,* how she takes herself. Her possessions signal her status as a woman to be envied:

Often a Woman is Judged by Her Possessions

There is a certain kind of woman who is born with an innate sense of style. She brings flair and originality to everything she does. For her Whiting and Davis designs marvellous handbags and accessories. Beautifully worked in extravagant mesh fabrics.

Carry a Whiting and Davis. Few possessions speak so well of you.

As above, suggestion is often made that one's possessions clearly communicate social status. They serve to protect their owners from risks associated with interaction with strangers, from having to do their own talking. As Georg Simmel recognized, money establishes a form of relation between people, and with it a relative freedom for the one who can buy and sell the other. Possessions then become a form of glamour capital which, in their sum, communicate that the wearer is among the especially privileged, the beautiful people. A perfume advertisement features a paparazzi-style photograph of a presumably extraordinarily wealthy European couple snapped off guard, with a bottle of perfume placed by the photograph. The copy reads:

SUBJECT:

Danielle, last seen in St. Moritz
Caution: It could be her double again
Man with her is Max, her bodyguard

COMMENTS:

One of the few things known about her is that she always wears Calandre

If Berger is correct that advertisements are fundamentally not about objects but about social relations, what social relations are implied in this advertisement? We, the audience, wish to know more about "Danielle." She wishes to know absolutely nothing about us. She hires a bodyguard to protect her from photographs, that is, from social interaction of the most minimal kind. She successfully maintains her privacy, remaining a mystery even to the prying paparazzi. She personified Berger's point that glamour provides a "solitary form of reassurance." She is separated from the attractive man in the photograph, the bodyguard, by reasons of class. She is separated from us, her audience, by reasons of glamour. Presumably, if we were to buy the perfume, we too could stand apart, untouched by the demands of others. We too could be envied.

The only way to be glamorous and *not alone* is to be alone with other glamorous people. This can only happen in glamorous cities and expensive resorts. It is no accident that the above advertisement is set in St. Moritz. One's being in a glamorous setting assures one's status as a bona fide player. With enough money, one has by definition the right to be there.

> If you happen to pass by 54 Faubourg St. Honoré in Paris, or by 54 via Borgognona in Rome, or by 177 Bond St. London or the Peninsula Hotel in Hong Kong, you will see Rossetti's shops and, of course, Fratelli Rossetti's shoes.

"If you happen to pass by. . . ." The advertisement implies the social relations. It implies in this case that the reader is no ordinary tourist; only a tourist would go to such famous shopping streets deliberately to stare at the windows, in Berger's terms, showing too much interest. The woman with beauty status and social status does not show too much interest; she is nonchalant. She happens to pass by because she is on her way to meet the mysterious Danielle for lunch. Or to confer with her investment broker. She is rich enough to have both business and pleasure in these exclusive locales, because she is an exclusive person. Rossetti's shoes can be found in less exclusive settings, "even in your city there is a shop." But, despite the evident condescension ("even in *your* city"), the advertisement goes on to reassure the consumer, "Of course, it is never an ordinary shop. Just as your way of walking is never ordinary."

The ordinary is that which must be avoided. It is that which will be transcended through the product purchase and subsequent rise in social status. *Ordinary* is an adjective used by advertisers only to indicate what their product is *not*. What their product *is,* by contrast, is variously "luxurious," "extravagant," "sumptuous," "rare."

> Raffinée. The instinct for the exquisite.
>
> Singular, sophisticated, sublime
> Mikimoto
> The Originator of Cultured Pearls.

The transcendence promised by beauty products is a promise of happiness. As Simmel recognized, there is a similarity between the psychological form of aesthetic attraction and that of money. Expensive goods that are beautiful in themselves, or that promise to make the woman beautiful, combine the psychological force of beauty *and* money, effectively doubling the promise of transcendence and the attraction: "for where else can the latter lie if not in the promise of pleasures that money can provide?"[6]

Those with high beauty status / social status search for this transcendence in the singular, the rare, the extremely hard to get. They demand and receive special treatment, because they are able to pay for it. Their beauticians and sales people are also part of the social relations of glamour. These people form the support system behind every glamorous woman. They are part of the implicit, if not always explicit, package. She has power over them; they execute her wishes. With their off-stage assistance, the on-stage glamorous woman transcends the everyday. She even transcends—advertisers would have us believe—the advances of age, ultimately death itself:

> Discover the "Special Beauty Secrets of Elegant French Women:"
> Discover Jean d'Aveze: a unique treatment collection from Paris, as effortless to use as it is effective. Part of the lifestyle of a certain genre of woman, whose breeding shows by the way she takes care of herself, the gentle, radiant, rose-petal way her skin looks and feels . . .

It is worth asking, here, why the advertiser uses the curious term *genre.* Is it to suggest that the rich are a different species, as separate from ordinary people as humans from the chimps? Or is *genre* to be understood as a different topic or type of painting? Are the rich works of art? The use of the term *breeding* does reinforce the emphasis on French elegance, but it is the elegance of pre-Revolutionary France. This elegance was available only to the aristocracy. Other adjectives heighten the emphasis on class separation. The clever use of *unique, secrets, effortless* indicate a lifestyle devoid of everyday stresses, a "gentle, radiant, rose-petal" way of life such as the aristocrats enjoyed before the peasants and bourgeoisie got out of control.

These advertisements live in a pre-Enlightenment world. They glory in privilege. They extend the contradiction that privilege shared by commoners (us) is still privilege. We can all be aristocrats, if we can afford the price tag.

Privilege, however, carries with it social duties. The duty of the beauty is to maintain her high status and to reflect that of her husband or consort. She cannot just play at it; she cannot just fool around. Her shopping trips are serious business. Her beauty maintenance program must take account of the latest advances:

> B21 Because there comes a time when every woman looks for a more serious approach in her beauty program. Orlane, with its great French heritage in the science of beauty treatments, developed Ligne B21 to go that step beyond the ordinary in skincare . . .
> Products that are not only singularly effective but of a quality to make them the choice of the most discriminating woman.
> Women with a certain maturity of taste who can be satisfied only with the finest . . .
> Ligne B21 fulfils all these needs—completely. With products of such elegance, such delicacy of texture, that they make skincare a pleasurable experience as well as a beauty necessity. In a range so complete, you need never settle for less than B21 to fulfil your skincare needs.
> Orlane: an advantage shared by the world's most beautiful women.

In this example science is married to history. The woman who uses B21 enjoys the advantages of both "great French heritage" and "the science of beauty treatments." She joins a highly select group of "the most discriminating women"; she partakes of "an advantage shared by the world's most beautiful women." While flattering herself (and being flattered by the advertisement) that she is being "serious," she can have sensual needs fulfilled. The first half of the advertisement legitimates the second half. The woman using B21 will have her needs fulfilled "completely" as she loses herself in its "delicacy of texture" and the "pleasurable experience" afforded. She need "never settle for less."

Products do more than establish relations between the self

and others. The act of ownership is itself a relationship between self and product. The purchase of products establishes a realm through which we can achieve what Simmel termed the "articulation of the self." This represents a form of freedom of expression, as we say *even to ourselves* who we are by what we have.

> Ownership is not, as it superficially appears to be, a passive acceptance of objects, but an acting with and upon them. Ownership, however comprehensive and unlimited, can do with things nothing other than provide an opportunity for the will of the Ego to find expression in them. For to own something, actually means that the object does not resist my intentions, that they can prevail over it.[7]

With many beauty products and services, the relationship established is one of pampering, in which the woman, with the aid of the product, creates a feeling of special care and luxury presumably lacking in her relations with others. Elizabeth Arden says, "You're in another world . . . when you come through the red door of Elizabeth Arden. And that world is based on one exclusive object—you. Whatever *your* needs or the time *you* have on *your* hands." If you do not have the time or the money, you can still buy Oil of Olay and "experience the feeling of richness as it gently penetrates. Soothing and smoothing away tiny dry lines with its creamy caress. Set aside a special moment with Oil of Olay Beauty Cream. And indulge yourself in the luxurious touch and younger look you'd expect from Olay."

To be the object of attention is a role in which women have often been placed, not actors but acted upon. While some women rebel against this role, others appear to objectify themselves one important step further. They turn their very bodies into advertisements. Perhaps because being a status symbol is such a solitary state, the hope is that one can avoid being alone by wearing or carrying a designer's name or initials. Such designers' logos may serve as modern-day crucifixes, protecting their wearers from encounters with ordinary men and women.

Thus it is that among perfumes the potential associations of a particular smell are frequently ignored in favor of a status name, a designer name. Giorgio proclaims itself "The Best-Selling Fragrance in Beverly Hills" and directs would-be customers to its *unlisted* toll-free number. The perfumes of Oscar de la Renta are advertised as being "as elegant, as sumptuous as the fashion Oscar de la Renta is known for." Similarly:

> Estée is the fragrance with the most exceptional of qualities: presence.
> And only one woman could have created it.
> Estée Lauder

Here the consumer is asked to identify with Estée Lauder as a successful feminine woman, the only woman who could have created a perfume with presence, who has presence herself, and who will presumably confer that presence onto the customer. In another advertisement, the copy gives the reader not a woman to identify with but a lifestyle:

> Bill Blass perfume
> is the cocktail party Blass
> is the tennis Blass
> is the dining out Blass
> is the New Year's Eve Blass
> is the night-we-called-it-a-day Blass
> is the stunner of a fragrance for women
> called Bill Blass.

This perfume clearly calls on the recognized social relations of the upper-middle-class wife, who supposedly spends a good portion of her time playing tennis, drinking cocktails, dining out, and celebrating her good fortune. Designer appeal can also be packaged in a more "affordable fragrance," as in:

> Oleg Cassini's world
> A world of uncompromising elegance and style
> expressed in these, the signature fragrances of Oleg
> Cassini.
> His is dangerously masculine.
> Hers is delicately floral
> And now, Cassini's world is brought to you by
> Jovan
> So it doesn't have to cost the world.

In this advertisement, Oleg Cassini offers more than a lifestyle; he offers a world view. His world is that of "uncompromising elegance and style." His world is one in which men are "dangerously masculine" and women are "delicately floral." What, one may ask, does it mean today to be "dangerously masculine?" What does it do for the woman, and to the woman, when he is dangerously masculine and she is delicately floral? To say the least, does it not subtly (perhaps not so subtly) reinforce and legitimate male violence as desirable and necessary to seduction?

Thus the language of beauty orders the world, reaffirming elegance, status, and style, reaffirming masculine and feminine stereotypes. In these advertisements designer names function as heraldic devices. On backsides and pouches they are status crests, announcing one's allegiances. They become symbols of consumer virtue and consumer honor.

This honorific competition is most apparent in advertisements for prestigious leather goods. Firms such as Hermès and Gucci encourage women to adopt as their own the initials of the manufacturer. In so doing, they adopt the techniques of historical narrative, reaching into the past for a referent by which to justify present status claims:

> In 1920, George Vuitton introduced a collection of handbags and personal accessories to complement the luxurious luggage created by his father.
>
> The "Carouchiere," entirely lined and detailed in leather, retains the spirits of the traditional French shoulder bag.

Luxury and tradition are woven into the LV initials. They are available at all the right addresses: New York's upper east side, Bal Harbour, Paris, Nice. Unfortunately for status seekers, the LV initials are also available on New York's lower east side, and for a fraction of the price. This is not the real version of course, and cheap imitation designer goods have caused an outcry among manufacturers. Wearing the LV initials but not paying the LV price is rather like appropriating the arms of a noble family, a false claim to privileged status that must not be tolerated.

Logically enough, what is inside a handbag should carry out the impression made by the exterior. Many major designers offer signature wallets and purse accessories. St. Thomas reassures consumers that "luxury loves company," encouraging them to buy its many small leather items. Rolfs places its monogram on each product to assure the consumer "of the ultimate in fashionable leather accessories, all created with painstaking attention to quality and craftsmanship. . . . No matter which you prefer, you'll be admired as a woman of exquisite taste." Again we see reference to the importance of social relations, of one's receiving the admiration and envy of others. All this work done, and money spent, so that the woman

can be admired for her taste, whether innate, as some advertisements suggest, or acquired by reading other advertisements
and following their advice.

Given the widespread desire to be envied in our individualis-
tic, competitive society, designer names are now appearing in
the most unexpected places: pantyhose, bedsheets, even boxes
of chocolates. Some advertisements, however, do not need
reference to designer names, any more than they need tout the
particular distinctions of the product itself. Like Simmel, they
recognize that money itself has become the ultimate standard by
which all objects are to be judged. So why not cut right to the
heart of the matter? Why not make money itself both signifier
and signified?

> Revlon says there's nothing better than:
> LOOKIN' LIKE A MILLION
> The roseywineryplummyberry shades guaranteed to en-
> rich your lips and nails, cheeks and eyes. Even the names
> sould like a million bucks: Plum Sable, Billionaire Blue,
> Million Dollar Wine, and lots more . . .

Another Revlon campaign is called "meanwhile, back at the
ranch." It features an exceptionally wealthy looking woman
sitting outside a southern mansion. Her staff of seventeen is
lined up dutifully behind her. Such are the social relations of
status, models for them provided by such popular television
shows as "Dallas" and "Dynasty." The latter itself provided
inspiration for a perfume, "Forever Krystle," and Linda Evans
is now selling hair color. "Dynasty" also suggested the model
for another line of makeup colors:

> Only Revlon would have the nerve to flaunt such a rich
> and restless collection of colors. Influential colors, Good-
> girl-gone-bad (but not too bad) colors. Like Private Stock

Brandy, Big Deal Blackberry, Wine Dynasty, Plum
Rich . . .

To some extent, working-class women may have an advantage over middle-class women as they face the business of
buying beauty products. If a middle-class woman is buying
status, she pays for it in part by not knowing how much it is
going to cost her before she commits herself to the purchase.
When lower-priced beauty products are sold in pharmacies and
discount stores, they are presented with prices visible, making
comparison shopping possible. More expensive lines sold in
department stores are each encased in their own special display,
well protected from contamination by the less prestigious lines.
They are also protected from the customer's comparison
shopping and informed buying. When a woman approaches the
Halston or Calvin Klein display, she has little way of knowing
ahead of time if there exists a difference in price or quality. With
little knowledge, she commits herself to the brand, a commitment often based largely on advertising appeals. On this level
women rarely comparison shop. In appearing to concern herself
over mere pennies where beauty is concerned, the woman
customer would be losing face, or status, rather than gaining it.

In the early decades of this century, wearing obvious makeup
marked a woman as cheap. Today, wearing cheap makeup
marks her as cheap. Virtue is associated with product alle-
giance. Great importance is placed on customer loyalty and with
customers' purchasing a whole line of products instead of one
single item. Ideally, companies would convince women they
need a whole wardrobe of makeup colors to match an equally
extensive wardrobe of clothes:

For soft city tweeds, a gently rounded face look
and delicate "Rose Tremière" lips.

With urbane suits, a soft-edged geometric face
contouring and pale "Beige Sellerie" lips.

Tailored casuals are gentled by a natural looking
makeup and burnished "Boiserie" lips.

For sophisticated late-day dressings: deep, dramatic
shadowing "Mauve Cheverny" lips.

The wardrobe suggests a lifestyle, a 1920s life of the middle-
class lady, her closet packed with soft city tweeds, urbane suits,
tailored casuals, and fancy late-day dresses. This image cor-
responds little with the active work lives and more practical
wardrobes of many contemporary women.

Along with the actual product, the packaging must reinforce
the status relationship between person and product, between
owner and others. Cheap bubble bath comes in big plastic jugs
like dishwashing liquid. Expensive perfumed bath silk comes in
small, delicately shaped vials. The first is secular, banal. The
second is sacred, mysterious. The first promises bubbles and
some cleansing; the second promises a veritable garden of
delights. There is magic in such bottles not unlike the magic
contained in other intoxicants. Bottles of perfume are like
bottles of alcohol. Each bottle is slightly different, each promises a slightly different experience. One could hardly label a
perfume "Bourbon," but one could, as Yves St. Laurent did, call
it "Opium" and get away with it, despite protest by those all too
familiar with the effects of the real substance and with the limits
of fantasy. As with opium pipe or bottle of Scotch, perfume's
packaging plays an important part in the ritual of indulgence and
separation from everyday concerns. The object itself, quite
apart from the substance, becomes endowed with magical
properties and appeal:

Even the classic lalique crystal bottle carries an unmis-
takeable message that the whole world recognizes.

. . . a perfect piece of sculpted jewelry, contoured in
the shape of Oscar's abstract flower in golden tones with
silvery stroke.

The emphasis on packaging as signaling the high status of the
product, the social status of the purchaser, extends to the
distinctive packaging used by major stores and boutiques.
Department stores such as Bergdorf Goodman's, Saks Fifth
Avenue, and Neiman Marcus all have their distinctive shopping
bags, which are a form of status advertising. Hermès ran a
series of advertisements focusing not on what it sold, but on
how it sold it:

Hermès is unique. Unique in Paris and unique in the
world. Unique in 1837 and unique in 1982. Just the sight of
a Hermès distinctive orange box makes one's heart beat
faster. Hermès means the best materials in the world. It
also means a certain style, a certain "savoir faire." . . .
And all this awaits you each time you untie the ribbon of an
orange box from Hermès.

Thus it would appear that women's role in conspicuous
consumption has continued, perhaps intensified, since Thorstein
Veblen wrote his famous analysis in 1899. As suggested earlier,
Veblen perceived how the social function of the lady was to
display herself as a privileged and leisured creature. She
demonstrated to the world the productive power and accumu-
lated wealth of her husband. The need to maintain at least the
semblance of work, of productive activity, limited his visible
consumption. She, on the other hand, consumed for him.
Draped in furs, loaded with jewels, she herself became a status
symbol:

The wife, who was at the outset the drudge and chattel
of the man . . . has become the ceremonial consumer of

goods which he produces. But she still quite unmistakably remains his chattel in theory: for the habitual rendering of vicarious leisure and consumption is the abiding mark of the unfree servant.[8]

In many earlier societies laws existed telling each caste or status group what it could and could not wear. In premodern China only the mandarins could wear fine silks and furs; in Elizabethan England only the aristocracy could wear the color purple. With the assumption of a mobile class structure, such legal strictures tended to lose their significance as a form of social control. As Quentin Bell argues, outward appearances then become regulated not by law but by fashion.[9] Fashion itself becomes a powerful form of social control. Fashion dictates who shall wear what based not on aristocratic birth but on supposedly democratic wealth. If a woman can afford it, then by all means she should, she must, buy it and wear it. Enjoy.

In its social consequences, this democratic fashion ideology may be more oppressive than were the earlier statutes. The Victorian lady's maid could and had to separate dreams of splendid luxuries from the harsh realities of her class position. Today, a poorly paid clerical worker is told by beauty and fashion advertisements that she has a democratic right to whatever she desires, that she too deserves to be envied. Moreover, she is told that spending may be the secret key to achieving status, beauty, self-worth, social approval, and love. But not everyone can achieve beauty status or trade it for a higher social status. Dreams rarely come cheap, social class is rarely so readily changed, the transcendence promised by advertisements seldom so easily won.

SEVEN
The Geography
of Beauty

The geography of beauty has its own time and space. It occurs in a world far different from the mundane one in which we live. It provides a suitable setting for beauty; it is both backdrop and reward for the successful performance of the beauty role. One cannot, for example, be glamorous in a sandpit. It is hard enough in Des Moines.[1]

When beauty redraws the map of the world, it enlarges some countries, leaving many others out altogether. If there is a hub to its universe, it is France, especially Paris, fashion capital. The names Chanel, Yves St. Laurent, Dior recall this centrality, as does the pervasive use of French ("Chanel introduces double couleur" . . . "Be the best you've ever been with Creme de la Blonde!"). Paris itself is thus a highly appropriate setting for beauty performances. In one advertisement an elegant Parisienne with a fur slung casually over one arm and a hat perched on her head strolls in front of a cafe. The copy is a question:

> Was it at Le Grand Cafe or some other wonderful place
> that we saw someone wearing the most marvellous shades
> of plum, red, fuchsia and magenta?

More likely the supermarket. But the invitation is extended to
the reader to picture herself being noticed, to play at sophistication, to see herself walking down the famed *boulevards,* or
sipping espresso in some chic cafe.

It is not just Paris, though. It is every part of France that
conjures up elegance, historic wealth, and class privilege. As
above, makeup lines in particular are linked to attractive French
regions and resorts:

> There is an undercurrent of excitement. . . . The anticipa-
> tion of the chase, and after . . . romance and intrigue.

Forêts Royales

> Orlane recreates the spirit and splendor of the fabled
> hunting parties of the French Court with Forêts Royales,
> for lips, eyes, cheeks and nails.

In the last advertisement the wealthy woman with her chestnut-
colored mane stares confidently at the reader with what John
Berger has identified as the stare of glamour, which looks "out
over the looks of envy."[2] She is presumably to be counted
among the hunters, not the hunted. A second example, also
from Orlane, similarly encourages American women to imagine
themselves in another hangout of French royalty, the lovely
Loire Valley:

> Orlane gave to its new autumn makeup shades a name
> that reflects the spirit of its creation: Chateaux de la Loire.
> The soft light of the Loire valley will play on your eyes,
> on your lips, your nails, your cheeks.

And the pale beiges, pink browns, the deep rusts compose a refined palette which will underline the strict elegance that fashion will impose this autumn.

Here we see again the use of the *passive imperative:* "the strict elegance that fashion [not designers, not advertisers] will impose." Obeying this voice of authority, the military-looking model demonstrates strict elegance in her sharply cut red hat and white suit. Her eyes look straight forward; she is at attention. In still other advertisements, the playgrounds of the international rich, past and present, become beauty backdrops: Deauville and the Riviera among them.

From France, one moves outward, as if on tour: next stop, Italy. From Tuscany come face masks bearing "the legendary restorative powers of Terme di Montecatini," from Rome, the perfume Fendi ("The passion of Rome is yours . . . now. The passion of Rome is Fendi, a new and compelling fragrance."). From Venice, more makeup colors:

Estée Lauder invites you to the splendor that was, that is, that will be forever

THE VENETIAN COURT COLORS

a renaissance of richness for eyes, lips, cheeks, fingertips.

Three separate photographs show the model, first, in opulent evening dress, then in a well-cut suit and holding ancient manuscripts, and finally in a fur-collared coat outside the famed Duomo. Western civilization and culture are equated with beauty products: Venice, its Renaissance, its riches.

Switzerland is famous as home not only to sanitoriums. Rather, its invigorating mountain climate seems to have inspired skin clinics for the fabulously rich, whose secrets are now available to those in the flatlands. Estée Lauder offers its Swiss

Performing Extract to the middle-class masses. More for the
frankly wealthy is La Prairie, whose advertisements ask, "What
Price Perfection?"

> Here, for you, is a new and unique range of precious
> skin-care preparations—La Prairie. Named after the ex-
> clusive Swiss clinic where in 1931 Dr. Paul Niehans
> conceived the revolutionary technique of live cell therapy
> . . . After years of research scientists . . . have per-
> fected a way of incorporating these cells into La Prairie
> beauty preparations.
> The La Prairie skin-care range, if regularly used and
> gently massaged into the skin will help to preserve its
> youthful appearance.
> For the woman who seeks nothing but the finest in skin
> care, there is only one answer—La Prairie—the secret of
> a lifetime's quest for beautiful skin.

If the answer is La Prairie, the question is not simply how to
look younger but how to look better. *Better* connotes more
glamorous and superior, better than others, just like the
jet-setters who patronize the Alpine clinics themselves.

Moving from the continent to the British Isles, advertisements convey upper-crust status through Cover Girl's
"Cambridge classics," makeup shades designed to complement
"roomy tweed jackets, argyles and soft felt hats." Such status is
also signified in Estée Lauder's Country Manor colors:

> Come enjoy vibrant cutting-garden-colors . . . antique
> colors—a season filled with rich gleaming new brilliance
> for eyes, lips, cheeks, fingertips. You are cordially invited
> to live in Estée Lauder's Country Manor Colors for the
> whole season. Do stay longer if you like.

The consumer may also escape all national boundaries. She
can take a cruise: "From Milan to Paris to New York to

you—Estée Lauder interprets the color signals from the fashion ports of the world and brings you her new TRANSATLANTIC COLORS." Though she is free, then, to picture herself in Paris or Rome or in the attractive countryside (English country estates, the hills of Tuscany), she is unlikely to picture herself in the less attractive areas of Western Europe (much of the Iberian peninsula, the industrial Rhineland, Normandy's dull potato fields, modern Belgium). Further, she is highly unlikely to picture herself in Eastern Europe. It is not fashionable.

Eastern Europe is too dull and oppressive, but much of the Third World, though poor compared with Western Europe, can at least be presented as an exotic paradise. "Look how hot color looks now":

Return to Paradise

> This spring, let Avon take you to Paradise
> Where the hottest colors are pulsating now.
> Blue Lagoon.
> Jungle Melon.
> Passion Flower.
> Colors so hot,
> they can only be from Paradise.

Warm-weather resorts, the West Indies in particular, often serve as backdrops for modeling summer fashions. This provides the opportunity for advertising tie-ins among the resorts, the airlines, and the products modeled.

Western beauty also feels free to exploit the natural riches of the world: beautiful woods and ivory from Africa ("The African influence surfacing in safari resplendence. Ivory creme. Gold satin. Tribal treasures stylized by Jay Feinberg") and silks from the Orient ("The Tea Silks. Revlon's luxurious and tawny hues for Spring"). Such advertisements draw upon the psychological confounding of the exotic and the erotic. They see the rest of the world through Western glasses—in this case, surely,

designer ones. Rarely does politics figure in—rarely, not never.
An advertisement for True cigarettes shows a muscular male
journalist with his typewriter perched on an orange crate,
surrounded by roosters and oil drums, waiting the next boat
out:

> *When you've been there and back*
> Dateline: Central America:
> "River of No Return"
> Update to Editor:
> Didn't find rebel leader. He found me!
> Story crackles with more intrigue
> than a spy novel. Back to capital
> when boat comes.
> (If crocodiles don't eat it!)
> P.S. Bring more True.

This is as close as we come to Third World politics. It is
important that the journalist in this sticky spot is male, not
female, that the situation is more a comic adventure than a
life-threatening assignment, and that the actual politics are
unspecified. We fill in the blank according to which side we are
on.

The only other time international politics intrudes is when
comic use is made of the Soviets. Their crime? Being unfash-
ionable. A Dep hair treatment advertisement shows a trendy
American girl being shown the route back by two stolid
uniformed female Russian guards. The girl, of course, is being
"Dep-orted."

Within the United States itself, certain states and regions
lend themselves more to the beauty treatment than others.
There is little that can be said for New Jersey or Delaware.
There is a lot that can be done with the visual drama and historic
myth of the West:

GO WEST YOUNG WOMAN, GO WEST

To find your best new shades of the season . . .

WILLI WEAR

Now Willi's put his brand on the best of the New West. A Santa Fe new mix of chain stitch skirt . . .

Freego: Denim Duels with Destiny

It's high noon, and as you walk down your main street there isn't a man around who is safe. You're smoldering under the sun in white-hot denim. You're glinting like a pearl-handled pistol, as light shards shoot from your bejeweled presence. Ah yes, the hero wore white, but now, so can the villain, thanks to Freego's denims.

In Reagan's America, it becomes easy to confound the West—its ready freedoms, its homegrown pride and optimism—with America itself. Lady Stetson perfume, set against the big sky, is "All American." So, too, is the idealized consumer: "Lady . . . you're free! Country proud. Playing in the big leagues . . . All-American. Lady Stetson. Every other woman in the world wishes she were you." Besides the wide open Western imagery, the baseball imagery ("big leagues," "All-American") suggests that wearing this perfume reflects one's pride in America, one's pride in oneself.

Urban–Rural

Within nations, advertisements have their choice of settings. Effective use is made of the urban-rural divide; glamour seldom happens in suburbia. To find natural beauty, logically enough, one goes back to nature. "Every color of hair has its own special glow. Uncover yours with Hälsa." The four long-haired beauties sunning in a meadow have presumably done just that with Hälsa Swedish Botanical shampoos and conditioners in four varieties. The brunette used walnut leaves, the blonde used marigold, the redhead ginger root, and the light brown-haired woman camomile. The back-to-nature theme appears frequently in advertisements for bath products, encouraging the consumer to leave the cares of civilization behind as she relaxes into her tub.

UNFORGETTABLE EVENINGS
BEGIN IN NORSCA

In the evening, especially after a hard day's work, come to Norsca. It's the perfect place to unwind.

A warm, luxurious Norsca Foam Bath has natural essences from the green forests of Scandinavia—to help you relax and get back in touch with yourself . . .

Come to Norsca. You'll feel better for it.

Kneipp Bath Botanics promise to "help you deal with the stresses and strains of our hectic times." Their hops bath "has been known for centuries for its calming qualities . . . it is particularly useful at bedtime." The rosemary bath will "leave one feeling invigorated . . . ideal as a pick-up either to wake up the system in the morning or to help one prepare for a full dose of work or play." The meadow blossom bath leaves one revitalized, the juniper bath soothes, the camomile bath aids beauty, and the spruce and pine baths lift the spirits. The benefits of a week in the country can thus be achieved through an hour in the tub.

The urban side of the dichotomy, by contrast, is concerned not with getting back to nature but with achieving sophistication. As Marchand has shown, advertising itself is urban-focused, as is the ideology of modernity that it promotes. City life *was* the life to lead, if one was to be modern, if one was to be glamorous, if one was to move with the times.[3] Today, with the perception of urban problems competing with the glamour of urban settings, this ideology is losing some of its power. But then even graffiti and garbage can give a *frisson* of excitement when juxtaposed to expensive fashions. The contrast suggests the wearer is urban hip—smart enough and chic enough to deal with inequality.

More often, though, fashion walks the main streets, not the mean streets, of major cities. Fashions are shown parading past cafes, boutiques, and restaurants where they are sure to be noticed. "In the Heat of the City, the Lady Keeps her Cool." And so she does, discoing in shiny evening gear, body and clothes protected by her deodorant. Liquor advertisements very often have an urban backdrop, as with the attractive black couple shown with their snifters—filled with rum—against the Manhattan skyline: "You may never drink cognac again." Glamour requires not simply that one drink, but that one know what to drink, that one have individual taste in alcohol, (albeit taste that is socially approved). Anthropologist Liza Crihfield Dalby has commented how different the Japanese attitude to drink is compared to the American and European. While the Japanese in the traditional setting drink sake, serving each other, Westerners must be individually served their private drinks reflecting their private tastes: "olive or twist?"[4]

Thus alcohol becomes a glamour accessory. Despite all the health warnings, it is still not chic to be a teetotaler. Except, perhaps, in California, which is a world of its own.

Beauty Time

Ultima II transports you to

Colors

far far away
The new fashion color
collection for spring

If it reminds you of anything you've ever experienced
or any place you've ever been, you must have had
a pretty good time . . .

As in the new physics, so too in beauty, time and space are
interrelated. One can hardly speak of one without calling up the
other. That many of these advertisements—Chateaux de la
Loire, the Forêts Royales, Venetian Court Colors, etc.—recall
past wealth hardly surprises. The opulence such advertisements promise hardly seems achievable in the modern age. It
seems more reasonable, then, to locate this fantasy somewhere in the past, to return to an earlier age, to, as the
advertisement says, "conjure visions of more subtle times when
luxury was still a viable way of life . . . when Kings still ruled
quaint kingdoms, and the world was a trifle less worldly and a
great deal more romantic." Escaping into the past, we are
encouraged to believe that luxury is less worldly than economy,
that the power of kings is subtle, and that romance is its
outcome.

Traditionally, men *made* history while women *were* legends.
The beauty of Helen inspired the Trojan War, that of Guinevere
forced the rift fatal to the Knights of the Round Table. During
the Kennedy Camelot, Jacqueline's fashionable beauty was
considered an asset to her husband. But when other first ladies
tried to play a more active role—Eleanor Roosevelt, or even
Rosalynn Carter—they were seen as meddling in the affairs of
state and, presumably, of men. The few women who exercised
real power in history—Catherine de Medici, Elizabeth I, Catherine the Great—fascinate in part because of the implicit threat.
What happens when a woman gains power, when a woman
makes history? For good or evil, the assumption is that she
must be exceptional, unlike other women. It is far safer for all,
then, when women are encouraged not to make history in their

own right and interest, but to inspire men to great actions, "all for the love of a lady."

Today, advertisements encourage women to identify with legendary beauties by purchasing assorted products that have been identified with their names. Western history serves as a symbolic lode that advertisers mine for the creative images they will attach to their products. The hope is that the mystery of the past will attach to the product. The veils of time truly veil the product in an aura of undying romance, transcendent beauty, and infinite youth.

Two perfumes are named after women. As is appropriate, both were dancers of legend: Isadora Duncan and Pavlova. The advertisement for Pavlova depicts an old-fashioned photograph of a dancer with the copy reading, "Pavlova, Paris, 1922. The Woman. The Legend. The Fragrance." Men build pyramids and fight epic battles. Women aim at love and look to the dancer, the female who scarcely exists apart from the romances she dances, herself the ethereal swan. Her life, as in the case of Pavlova, is rendered into myth. The few women who *are* recognized as forming part of political history—Indira Gandhi, Golda Meir— would hardly do for perfume labels. That they seem so inappropriate is not simply because they were not great beauties, but rather because their accomplishments were so significant that any advertising fantasy associated with them would be overpowered by their historic reality. Potential customers might then realize that there is more to achieving identity than purchasing fragrances.

Products other than fragrances use this technique of moving back into mythic time to evoke something lost, something that can be regained only through purchase. In makeup lines, advertisers similarly rewrite narratives about legendary beauties. The characters might be real-life or fictional. One makeup line called "Scarlet" featured a Vivian Leigh look-alike wearing what were described as "strictly sensational . . . strictly female colors." Another line called "Natchez" evoked a similar sensual image of the antebellum South:

> Live the legend
> Inherit the wind
> Discover . . .
> The elegance of America's
> most romantic era.

Such advertisements feed into the mythic understanding of southern women as more feminine than northerners. The myth of the southern lady and its impact on southern women have been tellingly described by writers and historians such as Shirley Abbott and Anne Firor Scott.[5] That behind the myth of the romantic South lies the history of the slave South is not supposed to concern the consumer. If Scarlett did not worry her head about it, why should she? Still, one wonders how many black women choose to identify with such marketing images. How many black women truly wish to "inherit the wind?"

The past offers more than legendary status; it also offers distinction. It validates. As Berger says, advertising cannot provide its own referent. It has to rely on something else. As I have shown, the resources of the wider culture are called upon to provide just such referents. One particularly effective source of validation is the "test of time."

NOW YOU CAN BE SLIMMER, YET
STRONG ENOUGH TO STAND THE TEST OF TIME

. . . Now, with help from new Fibre Trim with Calcium, you don't have to sacrifice strong bones for the sake of a slender body . . .

With a little help from Fibre Trim with Calcium, you can make extra weight a thing of the past. And still build a body that could make history.

While the copy is concerned with the woman's physique, present and future, the photograph poses a woman in a body-fitting white knit against a column of what looks like an ancient temple, thus moving back in time to assure the woman's beauty future.

Through identification with a tradition, a woman associates herself with people of known good taste, her own good taste becomes recognized in turn. She becomes both inheritor and ancestor. What she is, what she wears, becomes a classic. She probably chooses Ralph Lauren sweaters and jackets, she probably wears his perfume, Lauren, "the essence of a timeless style."

Besides becoming part of a legacy or a legend, there is a second way of achieving transcendence over time. It is the very opposite of tradition: it is living for the moment. If the traditional is associated with timeless beauty, then the transitory is associated with evanescent glamour. These are two dominant modes, two opposing ways of being beautiful.

The word *beauty* itself comes from the Latin *bellus,* a diminutive of *bonus,* or "good." *Glamour* is of more recent coinage, the responsibility for which can be traced to Sir Walter Scott and Lord Byron, who suggested the dark and sensuous woman as counterpart to the blonde and virtuous.[6] Social critic John Berger views glamour as linked to the development of capitalism and the element of envy associated with the assumption of a mobile class structure replacing the formerly rigid, caste-like divisions.[7]

But there is more to these modes than is revealed in their terms alone. Each has acquired additional connotations that, as suggested above, stand opposed to each other.

To begin, beauty can be seen as agrarian, glamour as industrial, or even postindustrial. The Hälsa women in the meadow with their fresly shampood hairdos are beautiful, not glamorous. Writers speak of the untouched beauty of a peasant girl's face in the same terms they use to speak of a surprisingly good provincial wine. The quality of both girl and wine is linked to the quality of the *terroir*, each grows out of nature and yet rises above it. Beauty standards thus vary according to the meanings assigned by particular social grammars of what Ivan Illich terms "vernacular cultures." In short, each village or town maintains a slightly different standard in selecting its queen.[8]

Beauty's best time is daytime; its best light is daylight; it admits to contemplation, in brief, to the pleasurable combination of thought and feeling. The woman in the Benson & Hedges advertisement looks beautiful at the breakfast table, but she certainly does not look glamorous, with her hair loosely tied with a scarf and her state of careless *déshabillé*. She can take the time to enjoy coffee and croissant with her man; there is time for talk and friendly smiles.

Beauty is knowable. The "local beauties" and "great beauties" are to be found within the social structure, albeit at different levels. As a knowable commodity, beauty has social value. Writers ranging from Anthony Trollope to modern-day theorists of human capital have understood that beauty can be traded for fair market price. In *Framley Parsonage* Griselda Grantly uses her beauty to marry Lord Dumbello, but as his wife she will be called upon to play a highly specific social role. Her beauty does not allow her to escape the social structure of everyday life, but merely to achieve a higher status position within it.

Social psychologist Bruno Bettelheim has demonstrated how, on a deeper level, fairy tales, ranging from the violence of Bluebeard to the final reassurance of Beauty and the Beast, reflect the understanding that beauty, unregulated by society, is a disturbing, even destructive force, the chaos of sexuality. But when beauty *is* regulated by responsibility, it becomes a constructive and altogether social force, leading the individual through deepening interactions of body and mind, beauty and beast, to new adult roles and sources of fulfillment. Thus, whether or not beauty *was* truth, beauty had to *acquire* truth as moral knowledge if it were to achieve its rightful place in society.[9] As today's Ivory Girl, the beauty assumes a mythic posture in modern suburbia: it guarantees that at least something, someone, in our society remains virtuous and good, and beautiful.

Glamour is a different matter. As Berger suggests, it is most possible in capitalist societies and most readily produced in industrial societies. To have glamour, one cannot rely upon the blessings of nature alone. Peasants cannot be glamorous. Nor can one trust to the simple ostentatious display of wealth or superior status position. To be truly glamorous is to be translucent: gilt-edged, metallic, evanescent, dazzling. "Captivating. Scintillating. Positively electrifying! New Electric Musk. Spray it all over and create a few sparks of your own." The excitement of Impulse body spray is captured by the young model in gold lamé and heavy gold jewelry and by the bright spotlights in the background.

In contrast to the long-standing debate over whether beauty is or is not skin-deep, glamour is understood to lie on the surface. Even Marilyn Monroe boasted as to how she could put on and take off her Marilyn act at will, passing either unnoticed—or very much noticed—on city streets.[10] While soul may be beautiful, that which lies within, soul is never glamorous (although lifestyle, more superficial, may be, as in "Life Styles of the Rich and Famous"). While beauty varies by region, glamour increasingly follows the international standard, regulated only by money and marketing.

Like beauty, glamour offers the possibility of escape. "She's not going to marry the boy next door!" (Rive Gauche). But it is not, as with beauty, escape from one social role into another, but escape from all predictable social limitations, all boring role expectations. In the 1930s and 1940s glamorous movie stars offered women and men the promise of escape from the

Depression and then World War II, from the daily constraints
and fears associated with these events. Today, jet-setters, rock
stars, and fashion models have the most glamour because they
presumably have the most freedom; their lives resemble adolescent fantasies devoid of adult responsibilities. Their work, if
they work, appears to be play; the world is their playground.
Princess Stephanie, for example, markets her own swimsuit line
presumably because she could not find any swimsuits in Monaco
to suit her. She works not because she has to, but because she
wants to, because it amuses her.[11]

Beauty has not been replaced by glamour but continues
alongside it, as earlier social forms continue to exist next to later
developments. In the 1950s the wholesome charm of Doris Day
was contrasted to the scintillating glamour of Marilyn Monroe.[12]
Today, it might be Jane Seymour contrasted to Joan Collins.
While beauty can be located at any class level, it must be of form
appropriate to that level. The peasant girl who models herself
on the manor lady presents not a beautiful figure but a ridiculous
one. Today's beauties, whether found in small towns or soft-
focus advertisements, are presented as accepting the traditional
female role. To get their full market value, they should add to
the raw capital of beauty signs of social value through recognized beauty roles. They should compete to be cheerleaders,
beauty queens, and to pledge the best sororities. Only then will
prospective buyers know that what they see others see, that, as
wife, the beauty will indeed prove "an asset."

At first glance, the glamour girl, less firmly rooted in a
delimited social setting, appears less tightly bound by role
expectations. Glamour promises sexual excitements not altogether congruent with the married state. In market terms, its
acquisition is risky, better left to international playboys and
princes who can afford to play, win or lose. The glamour girl is,
however, tightly bound to a changing set of prescriptions and
proscriptions, many of which are communicated by adver-

tisements proclaiming what fashions and beauty trends are "hot." Glamour must always be new:

Zazu Colorburst.
Brave New Makeup for Your Hair

Don't you have a few wild streaks in you? We thought you did. So we invented mascara for your hair. 10 brush-in streaks of colour. Hair today, gone tomorrow. But the impact lingers on.

In addition, the glamour girl faces the problem of her own transience. For, while beauty wisely secures a stake in the social structure, traditionally through marriage to a powerful and wealthy man, the glamour girl, to remain on her shaky pinnacle of the enviable, must continually provide new proofs. She invests more—financially in wardrobe and makeup, more in time and the organization of her production of the self—for what are presumed to be the greater rewards of celebrity and fame.

Thus, though both the beauty and the glamour girl hope to achieve a form of transcendence, escaping time either through lasting tradition or short-lived fame, neither truly does free herself. The beauty is tightly tied into the social structure, into a well-defined web of social expectations (not the least of which is to be, and remain, beautiful). The glamour girl is equally burdened by the demands of both fulfilling and breaking expectations, of continually coming up with something new. As long as they are judged by appearances alone, they must devote their very lives to them.

Just as romance novels typically take place either in some exotic land or historic setting "long, long ago," so, too, advertisements find that the promise of their product gains by connection to some romantic time or place. This partly explains the disparity between the images of women in advertisements and the real women we know. The first are characters, acting out beauty roles in our imagination, drawing upon an array of historic and geographic images that have little connection to historic fact or geopolitical reality. The second are actual women who juggle complex roles, and who *work,* at home and in the labor force.

This is a critical difference. Characters never work, in the sense that they never put in any effort. Their clothes can be luxurious and impractical because they stand no chance of getting wrinkled or soiled; their makeups are perfect and refined because there is always time to reapply. Thus they not only do, but *must,* exist outside of time or space. We mortals, however, cannot maintain this transcendent state; for us, it is the here and now, whether urban, rural, or suburban. For us, the everyday is our home.

EIGHT
Woman in a Man's World

Many advertisements refer to symbols and imagery associated with what Jessie Bernard called the "female world," but others bridge the gap between it and what has been traditionally recognized as the man's world: wider participation in society, economics, and politics. They accomplish this bridging through the clever use of puns.

Puns are not unique to women's advertisements; rather, as suggested earlier, they form an essential part of advertising rhetoric. Their bridging motion from one sphere of activity to another often incongruent one is, as suggested in Chapter Two on Madison Avenue's methods, a classic example of Koestler's description of the creative act. When the contrast between the two spheres is fresh, it benefits from the elements of shock and surprise. It captures our attention and, if the advertisement is effective, holds it while the visual presentation and copy sink in.

Thus the implicit comparison in the advertisement that proclaims "Comes The Revolution in Lips" ("Now . . . you wouldn't want us to start the revolution without you. Would you?") may be less fresh—and less effective—than another for weight control that draws a less-hackneyed comparison between the product and a historic political movement:

How Fibre Trim Gave New Strength to the French Resistance.

The photograph shows a stylishly thin Frenchwoman walking speedily past a French bakery window filled with exquisite pastries. "Take a cue from the food-loving French, and boost your will power with a little help from Fibre Trim. Vive la resistance!" Besides the attractive photograph with its visually interesting street pervaded by soft light, the association with the lasting glamour of participation in the Resistance is added to the fashion chic associated with France.

In the realm of economics women are promised "Social Security" if they use Head & Shoulders shampoo: "It's confidence that comes from knowing you may never see flakes again." They are promised economic savvy—"What Every Woman Should Know About the Oil Business"—with Corn Silk oil-absorbent cosmetics.

Through such advertisements the images, actions, and events of the broader world are translated into the more confined world of cosmetics and fashions. They offer vicarious participation of the least threatening sort; that is, we know it is not serious. We know it is only a verbal and visual joke. Such advertisements are meant to be fun. Like the femininity they proclaim, we are not supposed to take them seriously, any more than we are to take ourselves, or our efforts to make our mark on the world, too seriously. That would not be feminine. As Susan Brownmiller says, there is a world of importance placed on women's not losing their femininity. Some women, though, walk a fine line between traditional femininity and traditional masculinity. These women, once, were called New Women.

The New Woman

In her essay "The New Woman as Androgyne" historian Carroll Smith-Rosenberg traces the idea of the New Woman over several decades and at least two generations of young women. For the women who were the educational and occupational pioneers of the 1880s to early 1900s, what was new about being a New Woman was the claim they laid to rights of reason, autonomy, and achievements, rights that had previously been preserved for the male sex. "Eschewing marriage, she fought for professional visibility, espoused innovative, often radical, economic and social reforms, and wielded political power."[1]

As the twentieth century began to unfold, however, the implicit threat to the male monopoly on achievement was answered with opposition. The New Woman was criticized as "unnatural"; she confused the accepted divide between male and female with something androgynous, something combining characteristics of both sexes. With the spread of Freudian theory, especially with the popularization effected by Havelock Ellis, the message of these original New Women became twisted and lost to future generations. In their place, a new New Woman emerged. Her achievement lay not in liberating herself from the confinement of her separate sphere in service of the world of education, work, and social action, but rather in liberating herself from female sexual innocence, real or feigned. Under this second definition, the New Woman of the 1920s was no longer, as previously, a threat to man. Instead, she was his accomplice in modernity. No longer a challenge, she became a playmate. Her attempts at androgyny now took the form of amusing sexual games such as cross-dressing or smoking cigarettes. She now played at being male without substantially challenging male authority.

This transition from original intent to coopted form is necessary background to an understanding of the reemergence of the

New Woman in the 1970s. It is wrong to assert that corporate America has been unresponsive to feminism. On the contrary, it has responded in its own predictable fashion. Contemporary advertisements have endeavored to suggest to women that the two previous images of the New Woman—as moral crusader and sexual confidante—can now be rolled into one unconflicted role. Advertisements suggest that today's young woman can successfully storm the bastions of male power—Wall Street, medical and legal practices, government, science—without threatening their male occupants. Armed with such new slogans as "assertive, not aggressive," and new beauty charms (the magic briefcase), women can make their mark on the world without leaving a mark on their male colleagues and lovers. As Barthes suggests, all contradictions become erased, lessons from feminist history recede, new liberationist myths emerge to captivate hearts and especially minds.[2]

The New Woman of the 1920s may have been shocking in her day, but she was in fact a welcome creature to advertisers, who quickly recognized and encouraged her taste for the glamorous, the innovative, the modern. New Women were sold everything from silk stockings to cigarettes; they were there as advertising as an industry came of age and helped it grow.

Today, there's a new New Woman for advertisers, and her efforts at liberation similarly suggest new themes and cultural references. If old stereotyped identities of French hookers or fantasy heroines fit her like rusty armor, the New Woman identity flatters, applauding as it does not mere sexiness or romantic sensibility but contemporary skills at juggling social roles: executive, mother, lover, hostess. If anything is possible, everything becomes possible, if not simultaneously, then in sequence. In common parlance, it is known as "having it all":

> You're tough, you're smart, you're driven
> You're soft, you're warm, you're loving
> You go from day to night without missing a beat

You've become the person you were meant to be.
YOU'VE COME INTO YOUR OWN
In colors for your eyes, lips, cheeks and nails
Charles of the Ritz
Because you'd rather be yourself than anyone.

This advertisement plays on the fact that some women find the idea of liberation threatening. Maybe it is tough out there. Maybe people will oppose them. "You're not one of those women's libbers, are you?" Maybe men will not approve if they act tough, smart, and driven. To chase away such fears, Charles of the Ritz reassures women that they can also be soft, warm, and loving, in other words, all woman. The "cultural contradictions of femininity" are thus instantly removed.[3] A woman can be liberated and still maintain her femininity, still be desirable. She creates a visual display of conformity, dependency, and the absence of challenge, other than sexual. In this advertisement feminine conformity is signaled through the wearing of Charles of the Ritz makeup. The woman becomes both "herself" and a Charles of the Ritz woman, as it bestows its more complex identity on her underdeveloped one: "*Because you'd rather be yourself than anyone.*"

Chances are, however, that women who themselves are tough, smart, and driven would not be easily swayed by such appeals. The women susceptible to such campaigns are likely those who try on the costume of the liberated woman just as they might assume any other instant identity. The liberated image is coopted as the consumer is exploited. Similar advertisements can be found in magazines for black women. In one, the New Black Woman is described as:

COOL AND CLASSY

She's accomplished and fulfilled. She's
determined and enterprising. She's chic
and fashionable. She's attentive and thoughtful.

She's attractive and alluring.
She's discovered a secret of compatibility she
never knew existed . . . she's discovered
Fashion Fair. . . .
She's a Fashion Fair woman.

Such advertisements directed at black women make a mockery
of their struggles and achievements, of the determination and
enterprise many black women have demonstrated in working for
themselves and their families.[4] Now, along with being strong,
they must think about being attentive and thoughtful, attractive
and alluring. What is economic survival or achievement compared to being "compatible?" This advertisement in truth
reflects the conflicts to which black women are exposed in the
larger culture.

Such advertisements suggest that, with the right makeup, a
woman can be all things to all people, especially to herself. As
with sex and romance narratives, here advertisements suggest
that the consumer tell herself a story about a Superwoman, who
probably chooses Rive Gauche perfume (*"pas pour les femmes
effacées"*—not for self-effacing women) and wears a Nautilus
watch on all her adventures:

Because
a woman has crossed the Atlantic single-handed by sail,
has conquered Himalayan peaks, has soared to outer
space itself . . .
the day has dawned when we must add one superb model
to our collection. In tribute to the woman of today.

What, one wonders, did Amelia Earhart do without one? Or
those women who trained Navy pilots but were not allowed to
fly combat missions themselves? These courageous women of
yesterday, didn't *they* deserve a Nautilus watch? There have

been women pioneers throughout history; this is nothing new. What is new is that the agency now believes sufficient numbers of women will identify with these pioneers at least long enough and deeply enough to purchase these watches. What they do after that is up to them.

Other jewelry advertisements reiterate the same popular theme. "You sure know how to stick pins into that old feminine mystique," congratulates an advertisement for diamond jewelry. But, of course, it is the advertisement that is sticking pins into women's serious proposals for gender role change; it is the advertisement that is attempting to defuse the feminist mystique all while pretending to support it. Thus, for the liberated, "a diamond is for now." They are told not to wait for—or believe in—tomorrows. And so they gain a shaky confidence by applying Charles of the Ritz makeup, spraying Rive Gauche perfume, fastening Nautilius watches, and tossing a Buxton's Cal-Q-Clutch into their briefcases.

NOWADAYS YOU HAVE TO HAVE BRAINS AS WELL AS BEAUTY

Buxton's Cal-Q-Clutch isn't just an exceptionally attractive clutch, it's highly efficient. Within that beautiful, rich, full-grain leather exterior is a calculator in a specially-designed compartment for fast, accurate computations . . .

At Buxton, efficiency comes in all different shapes, colors, and styles—from our high-styled Cal-Q-Clutches to our other well-appointed Cal-Q-Secretaries, Cal-Q-Travelers, and Cal-Q-Pads.

The Cal-Q-Collection from Buxton. Isn't it great to look so smart?

This advertisement relies on the identity confusion between product and person, between looking smart and being smart.

Who is it that is beautiful, rich, and exceptionally attractive, all while being highly efficient, having, as the advertisement says, "brains as well as beauty?" Through the sympathetic magic of advertising, the characteristics of the object are transferred to the subject. A woman's possessions thus assume totemic importance; they speak for her and of her.

One of the most famous, and controversial, of this genre of advertisements was the Maidenform "I dreamed I was . . ." series. In one 1950s example the Maidenform woman dreamed she went back to grade school in her bra. In the early 1980s, though, she was no longer dreaming. Rather, she turned up: "The Maidenform woman. You never know where she's going to turn up." She turned up at a commuter train station: "She's going places in style in elegant, sensuous Delectables . . . Just what you've been waiting for." She turned up in a lion's cage: "She's always in control over the situation in slick, sensuous Sweet Nothings . . . In an array of spectacular colors." And she turned up reviewing the troops: "Her presence is commanding in elegant Chantilly . . . In a wonderful lineup of attention getting colors." She did not have to work or fight to get anywhere. She just turned up.

In other lingerie advertisements a new tone of realism appeared. In the end, however, it was but another dream of achievement with no femininity sacrificed, but all power gained. One advertisement pictures a young woman executive staring out the window of her spacious office, presumably overlooking Central Park. As Marchand demonstrates, the image of the executive looking out the window is a classic icon of modern male authority, here obviously claimed by the female.[5] A clear thinker herself, she is aware that:

> There are times when even the wisest decision may not be the most popular.

At times like that, how you feel about yourself can make all the difference in the world.
Vanity Fair
A little unfair advantage.

In another, a neat and prettily dressed woman looks stern—and out the window. The man standing behind her is perplexed. She too realizes that

Life isn't always fair. There are times when confrontation seems to be the only way to clear the air.
At times like that, how you feel about yourself can make all the difference in the world.

These advertisements draw on the commonly held assumption that a woman's beauty gives her "a little unfair advantage" in the business world. Reports from the field suggest otherwise. Women in businesses are discouraged from looking "too beautiful," from distracting both colleagues and clients by too obvious a feminine display. Another advertisement suggests that a woman save such displays for more appropriate times and places: "You may be a banker by day. But you're a woman by night . . . Live your life in Kasper." The modern New Woman juggles her identity as she juggles her wardrobe. She is feminine close to the skin, where it counts, applying makeup and wearing lacy lingerie. But out front she is all business, with her Nautilus watch and her Cal-Q-Clutch. Some products even promise to change their tone as she changes her role: a perfume, for example, that is serious in the boardroom but sensual in the bedroom.

If products emphasizing sex and romance offer the consumer brands of love-magic, then these liberated goods offer new forms of success-magic. It *is* difficult to succeed; there are no easy gains. The only "unfair advantages" are those held by Harvard men, not those held by women with pretty lingerie. This seems an obvious fact. But then the role of these advertisements is to turn consumers away from the obvious. In the face of the disheartening, they provide encouragement, even as they threaten to distract women from the other things they might be doing to achieve their goals.

You've Come a Long Way Baby

Cigarettes represent a major portion of advertising revenues in the women's magazines studied. Cigarettes also represent a source of identity, a social marker that includes several messages at one and the same time.

As smoking was originally taboo for women, cigarettes became associated with sexual daring and sophistication. In their early advertisements as they tried to develop this latent feminine market, the makers of Lucky Strikes called on testimonials from sophisticated Europeans such as society women, singers, and actresses who, presumably, were not held back by the parochial customs of small-town America. These testimonials did not simply promise sophistication; they also promised health, or "throat protection." As Russian dramatic actress Nazimova attested,

> The Russian lady—ah how she delights in the puff of a fragrant cigarette! As a Russian I have tried them all—the cigarettes of Cairo, Paris, London, Madrid—but here in my adopted country, America, I have found my favorite cigarette "The Lucky Strike." In addition to its lovely fragrance and wonderful flavor it has no bad effect upon my

voice—so even when I go abroad I carry with me my little trunk of Luckies—and enjoy a puff from America.[6]

In another major campaign Lucky Strike suggested women "Reach for a Lucky Instead of a Sweet." One advertisement depicted a slim and youthful horsewoman on her mount skillfully jumping her hurdle, while a black silhouetted figure of her possible fat future, complete with triple chins and sacklike form, loomed in the background. "Pretty Curves Win! When tempted to over-indulge 'Reach for a *Lucky* instead.' "[7]

In the early decades of the twentieth century, cigarette smoking represented one form of rebellion against adult authority, of announcing sexual liberation, and of claiming male privilege. It still does. The ages at which the rebellion occurs have slipped downward from the twenties into the grade-school years. But the advertisements still testify to this underlying assertion of a change in sexual status: from child to adult, from sexually constrained to liberated, from confined in a dull round of female chores to experiencing adventure as one of the boys.

When Marlboro cigarettes first appeared in the early 1940s, they were aimed at a female market. They failed dismally. So they underwent a change in gender. In rode the Marlboro man, and his powerful, hustling figure has been with us ever since. He sells to women as well as men. His image appears frequently in women's glamour magazines, now joined by the equally powerful downhill racer of Vantage cigarettes—"Performance counts. The thrill of real cigarette taste in a low tar." The woman who smokes can also ride with her man to snowy peaks to find "the experience you seek. Kent."

She can go it alone. She can "dare to be More," which, in the More advertisement, seems to be more long, more lean, more fashionable, and more masculinely attired in pin-striped trousers, checked jacket, and slouching fedora. That cigarettes have become a fashion accessory is clearly communicated by the designer cigarettes Ritz, "a celebration of style and taste by Yves Saint Laurent." The different Ritz advertisements each depict a slim, sophisticated model in evening dress, jewels, and cigarettes, with an attentive, attractive man waiting by her side or in the wings. Another brand, Eve 120's, comes in an attractive white and paisley package; it promises the woman who smokes it that she will be "every inch a lady." What a distance covered since the 1920s, when smoking was a sure sign that a woman was anything *but* a lady!

The best-known women's cigarette advertisements are surely those of Virginia Slims. They play upon the very idea of the New Woman, the visual contrast between old restrictions and new freedoms. The old restrictions are depicted in a small, sepia photograph across the top quarter of the page. "Virginia Slims remembers the first woman to enter the cold, cruel business world" (she stands frozen and forelorn, delivering huge blocks of ice from her Fenton Falls Ice Co. truck). "Virginia Slims remembers the first woman accountant. After she a'counted the cows, she a'counted the pigs" (the poor farm wife takes count of the limited livestock). "Virginia Slims remembers when a woman had the world at her fingertips" (what else?— the housewife dusts a globe in her husband's study).

Now, we are reassured, "You've come a long way, baby." The dull, sepia world of the past is contrasted with the multicolored present. Today's young women do not have to earn their bread through sweat. Nor do they have to take abuse from men. Today they are free to wear high-fashion styles, to smoke and to smile at their good fortune, especially if they can ignore the incongruous warnings under the photographed feet. "SURGEON GENERAL'S WARNING: Smoking by Pregnant Women May Result in Fetal Injury, Premature Birth, and Low Birth Weight." "SURGEON GENERAL'S WARNING: Cigarette Smoke Contains Carbon Monoxide." "SURGEON GENERAL'S WARNING: Quitting Smoking Now Greatly Reduces Serious Risks to Your Health."

It's a free country. The political battle raging between smokers and nonsmokers, between individual rights to smoke and group rights to clean air should make every woman stop and think. Which side is she on? If she smokes, is it worth the health risks? Advertisers counter the surgeon general's small boxed warnings of future pains with the promise of immediate pleasures. "Alive with pleasure! Newport. After all, if smoking isn't a pleasure, why bother?" The crew of happy, grown children careening down the snowy hill seems to have made their utilitarian equation and decided to live in the present. If you like to smoke, that is all that matters, suggests Benson and Hedges in its cozy domestic scenes of couples and groups, both single-sexed and mixed, all relaxing in good spirit and shared fellowship. "For people who like to smoke," reads the copy, "because quality matters."

Actionwoman

The French call her *la femme sportif* and point to the number of advertisements directed at winning her attention. British sociologist Judith Williamson calls it "the leg warmer syndrome."[8] It seems to be an international phenomenon, the way in the 1970s advertisers started picturing women in sportswear, especially leotards and legwarmers. What goal is served? The new freedom is translated into a new physicality, a new feminine toughness, void of serious commentary or political content.

In feminine hygiene advertisements in particular we find a contrast between the stereotyped appearances of Everywoman (traditional femininity) and Actionwoman (the new femininity, with legwarmers). Stay-at-home or sportswoman, such is the choice presented.

In the Everywoman advertisements there does seem to be rather a lot to do at home. A woman can do simple floor exercises—"now my period feels 3 days shorter." She can gaze at herself in a mirror, admiring both her slenderness and that of the new "Slendar" tampon. She can "be (herself) with Libra"; like the model shown she can cuddle up on the sofa and talk on the telephone.

In these advertisements if a woman works, it is usually at an appropriate "feminine" job. She is a student teacher. "Between taking classes and teaching classes, I like to feel my freshest . . . No matter how busy I am, it's nice to know I can always feel fresh." She is a model: "I have to feel this fresh all day, every day. My job depends on it." Best of all, she can be a mother, or even a mother-to-be. For, even if her periods have stopped, "Feeling this fresh all day seems to be more important than ever now." While in other advertisements women are sometimes portrayed in positions of authority, such is rare in sanitary product advertisements. Perhaps the old taboos of woman's emotional instability while menstruating make her less likely to be portrayed as a pilot, surgeon, or lawmaker.

Still, this does not confine *all* women to the role of Everywoman. Woman's supposed emotional instability can be channeled, if not into the challenges of work, into those of sport, where she will be responsible only for her own well-being, for her own body, rather than for those of others. An altogether less threatening prospect physically, socially, politically.

Actionwoman plays basketball and parachutes into trees. She favors a tampon for tennis. She engages in the highly demanding sport of downhill racing:

> When you're active, you really need the action protection of Tampax. Whether you're skiing, skating or just snowballing around, a Tampax tampon is protection you can count on.

Actionwoman was child-woman Cathy Rigby, Olympic gymnast:

When a four-inch balance beam is the only thing between me and the floor, I can't afford any distractions. So
I'm especially glad I choose Stayfree Maxi-pads.

Today she is Mary Lou Retton, selling not sanitary products but
sports shoes—and Wheaties.

The liberation of women and the rise of Actionwoman is
visually charted in an advertisement from Trendar, a product for
menstrual pain. Three photographs, increasing in size, move
from a picture of a young woman in an old-fashionned Peter Pan
collar and pink cardigan who is sitting in a stuffy chair and
looking definitely bored ("Since the 50s, menstrual pain meant
Midol"). The second photograph shows a long-haired nature girl
complete with fringed leather vest. Now she is standing, if still
looking bored ("In the 70s, it also meant Pamprin"). The largest
photograph shows the young woman of the 80s, in pink leotard
with white armbands and sweat band. Neither sitting nor
standing, she must be exercising; why else would she have her
hands behind her head? But she cannot really be exercising,
since she's smiling pleasantly ("Now there's TRENDAR Today's Choice for Menstrual Pain"). Today, Actionwoman is
Everywoman's adventurous sister and counterpart; she guarantees the limits so that the homebodies can feel safe and secure
within them.[9]

Along with sanitary products, deodorants confront the tension between the need for safety (Everywoman) and the desire
for strength (Actionwoman). But they resolve it in a different
way, by locating the two qualities within the same product,
assuring readers that their product is both strong (masculine)
and soft (feminine). The classic example is Secret: "Strong
enough for a man, but with the curved comfort for a woman":

Unlike hard-edged men's solids, Secret's powerful pH-
balanced protection is curved to fit a woman's underarm
comfortably.

The background is a black-and-white shot of a man's powerful fist clutching the hard-edged masculine deodorant; the foreground overlaid is a color photograph of a delicate, manicured women's hand (colors all soft skin tones, pinks and baby blues) that holds the gently rounded feminine deodorant, with a stylized flower above the brand name.

The old adage held that "horses sweat, men perspire, women glow." The new advertisements state forthrightly, "women sweat, too." The blond teenager in white leotard and legwarmers rests on the floor beside the ballet barre. Her antiperspirant, Lady Speed Stick, "protects you like a man, treats you like a woman." It too is packaged in soft colors, baby blue and white, unlike male antiperspirants, in strong primary colors and striking neutrals: blacks, browns, and golds.

Other product lines answer more directly Actionwoman's needs; she has to get the leg warmers and sneakers from somewhere. Such sports clothing, whether worn for sports or for shopping, has become a major part of the clothing market. There the advertising rhetoric is much more straightforward and serious, the sort of technical rhetoric usually reserved for products aimed at men:

> Stretch II body tight: Comfortable, 4-way stretch poly cotton Lycra, one-piece construction with T-back and double layer upper body for support. Air Performer aerobic shoes: Flexible NIKE-AIR cushioning system; exceptional stability; lightweight.

The wet-haired model is recovering from her workout, resting against a rolled-up mat in her red leotard and gray-and-white legwarmers. Unlike the Trendar maiden, this one is serious, as is the athlete in the Pony shoe advertisement, showing off impressive muscles while performing a handstand ("Perfection. In mind. Body. And Sole"). So, too, is the skier in the Nordica advertisement ("The ultimate comfort is our 2-way air fitting system").

Whether softly feminine or more assertively physical, these women are all after a form of perfection. As Baudrillard has commented, the concern people used to place over the state of their souls they now focus on the condition of their bodies.[10] The search is for personal perfection and for transcendence: once, eternal salvation was the goal; now, momentary high will have to do.

> Fresh winter air.
> A long deep breath.
> Sheer joy. You plunge ahead.
> A silent glide down the side of a mountain.
> You've never felt more alive in your
> life. Today, no mountain is too big,
> No challenge too great.
> You've reached a new high in your NS 850.

NINE

The Accursed Portion

> When you suddenly catch a glimpse of yourself in a mirror, you notice little lines. Dull-looking skin. You just don't look as young as you could.

Georges Bataille believed that society contains *la part maudite,* an "accursed portion," that portion which exists above and beyond the merely necessary.[1] I use it somewhat differently here to examine the attention advertisers focus on all those parts of the female body that they consider "accursed," useless, not necessary, and not attractive. Even the most casual peruser of women's magazines can hardly help being struck by how much critical attention is devoted to women's bodies, how much self-hatred is encouraged in advertisements that ask "Dark Eye Circles? Age Spots? Blemishes? Freckles?," that demand to know "Do You Shine Where You Shouldn't?," that command "Combat Aging Zones."

With the great competition to market successful new products, advertisers have embarked upon what I would term a "colonization of body surfaces." No longer should women simply moisturize their faces; now they are told to moisturize their whole bodies. Special creams for face and hands will not suffice; these have been joined by neck creams and breast creams and, of course, body creams. "Bumps and Bulges? Rediscover Shapely Contours":

> Pinch the back of your thigh, your buttocks or the calf of your leg. Don't despair if skin takes on a spongy, orange-peel appearance. This concern, politely referred to as "cellulite," is shared by 90% of women today. Lack of exercise, poor circulation, water retention, imbalanced nutrition and more are the reasons why!

"This concern" is polite language for *la part maudite,* this beauty problem our grandmothers did not know they had, if they had it. Now cellulite is the concern of 90 percent of women. The Victorian lady might be concerned lest too much leg show as she crossed the street. Today's young woman must be concerned lest too much "bikini hair" show as she tans on the beach. With more revealed, there is more exposed, not just to air but to commercial exploitation. Thus Pantene, for example, says it has "a message to every woman who thinks she looks younger with her clothes on." If the woman suffers, as suggested above, from little lines and dull-looking skin, there is still a solution, namely, "Spa de Pantene," to make "every inch of you smooth, silky and delicious to touch."

For young women, the problem is pimples, spots. Advertisers promise that social acceptance will follow upon the clearing up of acne and assorted pimples. Advertisements here assume the tone of a mother advising her daughter on proper skin care, with the language becoming condescending and simplified.

> A spot on the face is unsightly. And the sooner it's out of sight the better.
> Because PHiso-Ac is specially made to blend with the color of skin, it can hide a spot immediately. At the same

time, it gets to work on the spot, killing germs, drying it out and removing any excess oil.

Use PHiso-Ac, and chances are that only you will know you have a spot.

The language is down-to-earth; this is serious business. Cover Girl Oil Control Makeup promises "No shining . . . No streaking . . . No yellowing . . . No fading . . . No blotching . . . No caking . . . No fooling." These are all the things that can go wrong with a girl's complexion; these are all cause for cursing, for lamenting one was ever born. In such a state, the best defense is a good offense. "Choose your weapon," instructs Noxzema, with products that will help wipe out acne ("Acne 12. The drop that can make it stop").

But one is hardly out of one's teens and over these facial traumas of youth, before fears of age set in. Much of the self-hatred engendered by advertisements is directed toward signs of aging, as in "phase out the aging look of dry skin," or Ultima II's Anti-Aging Firming Foundation ("Makeup Assumes A New Responsibility"), or model Jennifer O'Neill, for Cover Girl, asking, "Is your make-up keeping up with the needs of your skin?" Special products help one to "combat the sagging around your eyes. The lines around your lips. The delicate zones that age first." Beauty treatments for face and body promise to "virtually reverse the effects of age on surface skin."

But, of course, it is not just skin. Every inch of the body must receive elaborate attention. With the tone of some well-meaning but obnoxious busybody, Sally Hansen asks, "Shouldn't you take care of your nails as well as you take care of your skin . . . Beautiful nails are as much a part of your beauty statement as your hair and skin, so, don't they deserve the same care?"

But the problem is not just with one's hair, eyes, lips, cheeks, nails, and so forth in this "baroque elaboration of body parts." The problem, more profoundly, is the whole body, the female body.

Kim Chernin calls it "the tyranny of slenderness." She sees in our national obsession with dieting not just a rejection of the overweight as unattractive or unhealthy, but a greater, more fundamental rejection of the feminine and, especially, the maternal. Dieting becomes the necessary entrance fee paid for social participation for women, especially in heterosexual relationships. If want ads for single men stress *tall* and *successful* as the desired attributes, then over and again the key words for women are *slim* and *attractive*. Fat people are considered so far out of the social swim, according to both Chernin and Marcia Millman, that others treat them as though they were not even present. Fat people, says Millman, are seen as either over-sexed or undersexed, and the men who do fancy fat women are, by extension, seen as having weird sexual tastes.[2]

Today, an unnatural slimness is seen as natural. It is the norm to which women strive to conform; when they fail, they often hate their bodies for their perceived imperfections. Susie Orbach believes many women postpone achievement of their dreams until they first achieve the magical "right weight"; for them, life can be lived only by the thin. They speak of their "fat" self and "thin" self, the latter representing the "real me" struggling to escape from overweight. But when they do achieve their desired weight, they often feel an identity confusion. All the issues of self that have been long forestalled must now be addressed; all the accustomed excuses for inaction or social rejection must now be faced.[3]

Other women succeed all too well in this battle. These are the anorexics, usually young women, who take dieting to the extreme, sometimes to death. In *The Obsession* Chernin calls them "hunger artists" and demonstrates how weight symbolizes their rejection of adult womanhood, their desire to establish their own control over the world, even if that control is limited to their own bodies. In her later book, *The Hungry Self,* she takes these arguments another step further. Asking why anorexia has reached epidemic proportions only in the past fifteen or twenty years, she finds the answer in the contemporary strains in the mother–daughter relationship. Today's young woman, especially when intelligent and highly motivated, needs to exceed the mother's life and achievements. Her mother, her original role model and teacher, ends up having nothing to teach her as she makes her way through to the new maze of opportunities. But, unlike the son, the daughter lacks a culturally legitimated means of leaving home. She needs to exceed and hence move away from her mother but fears doing so, fears rejecting the mother without having any clear future toward which to head.[4] Noelle Caskey disagrees, seeing in anorexia a desire to fend off the father. As she explains it, "anorexia results from a psychically incestuous relationship with the father." It both expresses that relationship and provides the daughter's defense against it, "an attempt to escape from domination."[5] In either case, the body appears as the one thing the girl can control; adult womanhood, the one thing she must evade.

Today, women are told, "You can never be too thin or too rich." As the number of anorexics rises, this statement loses its presumed charm. Still, as the media parades its slim models before women, many end up considering themselves five, ten, fifteen, twenty pounds overweight. By medical standards, which themselves are not uniform, some of these women are overweight, but others are only deluding, in some cases hurting, themselves. But many women would agree with Colette, who remarked, "Give me a dozen such heartbreaks, if that would help me to lose a couple pounds."[6]

This dedication is reflected in the advertisements, where losing weight assumes the seriousness of a religious quest. In the early 1980s four major diet religions have been competing with each other for followers. Each preaches a different creed; each proclaims a different good. The Pritikin diet originally relied on a spartan regime based heavily on carbohydrates, with very little fat. The Scarsdale diet, by contrast, treated carbohydrates as near-forbidden food and relied heavily on proteins. It follows logically, then, if not sensibly, that the third diet, the Atkins diet, was based on high fat intake.

In contrast to these three diet "religions," each advocating the benefits of one food type, Weight Watchers stresses a balanced diet of all foods. Jeanne Nidetch, founder of Weight Watchers, rules as its high priestess. She herself was originally "lost" to overweight but then found the way out through the Weight Watchers diet, which she shares with others. Her weigh-ins at Weight Watchers meetings are rituals of abasement and redemption, to which negative and positive sanctions are attached. Only those seriously in need, only the seriously overweight, are admitted to meetings and allowed to share in the full fellowship. Others may partake of the blessings through reading the Weight Watchers magazine and selecting meals from its line of frozen dinners.

Competing with these major diet religions are numerous food cults. Miracle diets are aimed in particular at working-class women, who often have neither the time to attend diet clubs nor the money for membership or for the relatively expensive diet foods. In contrast to the above stress on strict self-control, these plans often offer painless remedies: "Lose Weight while you sleep," "How to eat as much as you feel like eating and still lose weight." An advertisement not for a diet, but a device promises:

> You can lose up to 5 pounds in 5 minutes—5 inches in 5 hours. With Second Skin—The Space Age Slenderizer That Starts Erasing Extra Pounds and Unsightly Inches Instantly!

Such advertisements speak to every dieter's dream of transformation without work or suffering. "Shed Hundreds of Calories Daily Even if You Eat More!" Just as many religious sects and cults base their sacraments on sacred substances, in some cases wine, in other cases marijuana, these diet cults proclaim the mystical powers of certain foods or products. One can supposedly "turn sagging backside bulges into sexy rounded beauty" through the use of a "trimiciser." One can supposedly benefit from the discovery of a "centuries-old natural stimulant [that] can help you lose weight."

> Thanks to an ancient secret of a South American Indian tribe, you can now lose weight easier than ever before and enjoy eating less! . . . It's called Guarana, an organic natural dietary supplement that gives you the power to INCREASE YOUR ENERGY WHILE DECREASING DIETING BLUES . . .

None of these advertisements speaks of renouncing life's pleasures. Instead, one can "Lose Fat and Calories Even if You Eat More."

> These crunchy wafers are designed to help you to bring to a STOP the struggle of sticking to a diet . . . To bring to a STOP the necessity for torturous exercise.
>
> By simply eating a few of these delicious wafers before meals, you are taking into your body the ingredients that scientific research reports show not only to rid the body of more calories automatically but to automatically rid the body of more fat as well.

Advertisements promise the reader she can eat all she likes and "still come down 2, 3, 6, or even 10 dress sizes." She might, one warns, even "become too thin!" Some advertisements emphasize the magic of Western science while others turn to ancient Chinese wisdom, as in one that tells readers:

HOW TO RUB YOUR STOMACH AWAY

This weight loss method does not come from Western medicine. No, its source is the wisdom of the ancient Chinese sages . . . arrived at through literally 6,000 years of observation and study of the natural principles of healing. It is only now that this ancient wisdom of the body is becoming available to you.

Other advertisements offer testimonials. In one, John, a bank president, describes his old self as overweight, sluggish, and constipated. At age fifty-five he was ready to give up when his secretary pulled him back from the brink by telling him of special exercises. "By applying the exercise faithfully, he regularized his bowel movement, and lost 40 pounds."

Logically enough, the major diets decry the proliferation of these quick-weight-loss schemes. What all share, however, is periodic recourse to the language of religion. So, too, do the advertisers, who promise women they can enjoy "mayonnaise without guilt. All the indulgence, half the calories," or the "nice and not too naughty . . . Weight Watchers Frozen Vanilla Dessert." Another encourages women to:

> Drink to your wicked past,
> celebrate with a calorie.
> There's only one calorie in a can.

Edam cheese is described as a "heavenly body," candies are "sweet temptations." In magazines dedicated to slimming, some advertisements present case studies in which the dieter's life history becomes a parable of good intentions and wicked outcomes. As one example:

One evening, as Polly Morgan sat nibbling on a carrot, a vision appeared: tender slices of juicy turkey drenched in rich, velvety gravy over a mountain of sage-scented stuffing.

She knocked a chair over running to the refrigerator.

Next thing Polly knew, she was tearing the tin foil off congealed corned beef and sodden marshmallowed yams.

And you know what?

Ms. Morgan doesn't even *like* corned beef.

Magazine articles also rely on the testimonial approach to inspire readers. In reading such case studies, one is struck by the correlation between marriage and motherhood, on one hand, and becoming overweight, on the other. In one case, a woman recalls:

I was only 105 pounds—very light for my height of 5 ft 4 in. Then I met the man who was to be my husband and my weight started to creep up and up. Most people said it was contentment but I'm sure it was a change of lifestyle. I was going out much more and eating a lot of snack food.

In another case, a young woman, age twenty-seven, was nicknamed "Granny Rogers" because she looked twenty or so years older:

Looking back, I suppose my weight problems started with my marriage to Iain and having two babies in quick succession. Oh, that does sound ungrateful—particularly when I have a good, loving man and two beautiful sons. Of course, I don't blame *them* but I wished someone had warned me to watch my weight when I first got pregnant.

Motherhood is more than a state of mind; it is a state of being. And according to some scientists, it is often a state of being heavier. In *Fat and Thin* anthropologist Anne Scott Beller says that a woman's body will tend to put on weight with, and keep it after, childbirth, especially after repeated childbirths:

> Taken together, the three major hormonal triggers to overweight (insulin, estrogen, and progesterone) are probably a normal hazard of any pregnancy; but their cumulative effect over the course of several pregnancies may be ruinous for women with a special susceptibility to them. After two, three, or four babies, such a woman's metabolic and endocrine machinery will have mastered the unhappy capitalism of obesity, learning to make much out of little in the process.[7]

It used to be that a girl underwent a status and figure change as she moved from carefree adolescence into responsible motherhood. Her body reflected her new social position. She became the plump and jolly Mama dishing out pies and cakes, encouraging all around the table to have "just another piece." A lean and hungry woman was probably a malcontent. Young girls might be coltish; mothers were large and steady as field horses.

Now this has changed. A woman may show her love by baking pies but demonstrates her personal virtue by not eating any. Now "wives should always be lovers too," especially if they want to stay wives. For the suggestion is that other, young and slimmer women stand ready to take their places. Examples of diet achievers appear in advertisements such as the Diet Pepsi: "Now you see it . . . Now you don't," or, more blatantly, the consommé advertisement that pictured the rear end of a shapely blond in a swimsuit, with the warning, "How the competition's shaping up for summer."

If the question becomes "What's a mother to do?," the

answer has to be, "Spend money to lose weight." Advertisements take two essentially labor-intensive activities—eating wisely and exercising—and translate them into capital-intensive activities. Women are encouraged to buy themselves slim through a range of expensive diet foods, machinery, and assorted gimmicks.

Curiously, health—the leading reason men go on diets—is scarcely mentioned by these advertisements as a reason women should diet. Health runs a poor third to the social approval of one's male and female friends and the personal approval of seeing oneself looking good in fashionable clothes. The British consumer magazine *Which* conducted a survey that indicated that 58 percent of the women questioned, as contrasted to only 19 percent of the men, said they wanted to lose weight to look better in clothes. Whereas 76 percent of the men gave health reasons for dieting, only 39 percent of the women wanted to lose to improve their health outlook. With clothes figuring so high among female reasons for dieting, perhaps the belated creation of fashionable clothes for larger women will help introduce a saner attitude toward body image. American women are finally being offered chic clothes in women's sizes, often in special boutiques.

In addition, recent research suggests that the woman who eats wisely, exercises moderately, and still has a few extra pounds may be doing everything right and nothing wrong. According to recent findings, the body may have a preferred weight range based on heredity and habits fixed in childhood. An individual will be able to diet down to this range if he or she puts on weight in adult life but will have a difficult time losing considerably more weight and keeping it off. The body will tend to return to its earlier equilibrium.[8]

Although the term *glutton* has traditionally meant someone who overeats in a particularly vulgar and senseless fashion, Henry Fairlie believes that the chronic dieter shares some characteristics with the glutton. Each in separate ways denies the true pleasures of food—its beauty, its varied enchantments; each separates himself or herself from the pleasures of social life, of the shared enjoyment of the table and company. Each places himself or herself apart:

> This solitude . . . is partly a result of taking something in our lives, which has its appropriate place and value, and then lifting it out of place and exaggerating its importance to us. In the end, it is no longer a part of our lives, but takes the place of living.[9]

Chernin agrees with Fairlie that the inward-turning of the chronic dieter could be better turned outward. She invites us to join her in imagining:

> a generation of women bringing to the work of self-evolution the same devotion, the same discipline, the same dedication . . . they presently invest in their search for the perfect diet. . . . Imagine us shaping that new woman, dream of the future, out of the transformed obsessions that presently rule our lives.[10]

This is exactly the problem. It is not that attention to appearance is unhealthy, but rather the focusing of all interests and energies on it, to the exclusion of other efforts and causes, that makes us question the influence of advertising. The body manipulation and symbolic mutilation encouraged by advertisements can literally extend until they encompass a woman's whole life. The idea that there is something wrong with her body can seriously affect her sense of self-esteem and her ability to act. Instead, she turns inward on that which she can control and that which she must control. Following the advertisers' advice, she turns her body into a statement. She transforms herself into an advertisement for herself, a complicated sign to be read and admired.

TEN
Beauty Rituals

Rituals provide drama in culture, stylized moments apart from the everyday affairs of society. They reveal the values that we share, that hold us together as a people. A society without rituals denies itself not only opportunities for reaffirming and reenacting values, but also for inspiring further social action and cultural creativity.

In the advertisements rituals take on several forms. Among the most common are what we might call "private rituals." Putting on and taking off makeup, even bathing, assume a ritualistic pattern. Like rituals, they mark moments of change, as from day to night, or work to leisure, public world to private. They show the value we place on beauty, its care and culti-vation, and on the social approval that results from it.

An important part of these rituals is that they are meant to be hidden from the public eye. In the privacy of her bathroom the woman must daily reaffirm the value of personal beauty and reenact her hope that she will never grow old. A woman who, as the French say, is *soigneuse de sa beauté* (careful of her beauty) is by definition virtuous, at least on this score, and her participation in this ritual is respected. A woman who is not is profligate with her beauty. If beauty is a virtue, then its neglect is a private vice, with public consequences.

Thus, though such rituals are performed in private, they are not divorced from social participation. Rather, they are perceived as the gateway to it. They mark the movement from the natural state of the unwashed, unmade-up woman fresh from sleep to the cleansed woman prepared with her social face to meet her social world. Oil of Olay captures the sacred tone and values involved in this process in a glorious two-page advertisement with a translucent quality, glowing warm but soft tones of peach and cream, a dresser top, where the ritual is performed, a mirror, reflecting the transition and, of course, the symbol of Woman. As Marchand has perceived, the diffuse light from above is a technique used by advertisers to suggest sacred presence.[1] Here, it also suggests transcendent potentiality:

The ritual that helps you look younger.

It starts with one extraordinary drop.
A beauty fluid that penetrates quickly,
greaselessly restoring what every day takes away.
A fluid that brings back fullness to where even
the finest wrinkle lines appear.
A fluid that recreates the look and feel of
younger skin.
The ritual of Oil of Olay, it can help you
look younger.

Thus the key value of youth—this hope of transcendence over mortality—is reinforced both by the vision of the sacred and the language of transcendence: *extraordinary, fullness, recreation,* and *younger*—the last repeated three times. It is a visually beautiful advertisement, and a reassuring one.

At the end of the day, another transition is accomplished as the woman removes her made-up identity and relaxes back into a more, if not completely, natural body. Advertisements for bathing products recall ritual oppositions as they call up the impure body and the pure soul. Sylvia Plath once wrote,

> I guess I feel about a hot bath the way those religious people feel about holy water. . . . The longer I lay there in the clear hot water the purer I felt, and when I stepped out at last and wrapped myself in one of the big, soft, white, hotel bath-towels I felt pure and sweet as a new baby.[2]

In many cultures bathing is symbolically associated with spiritual purification, the washing away of former sins and identities in preparation for a new life. In Christianity the act of baptism in water was preliminary to acceptance within the community of believers. In many religions and societies it also symbolizes the discarding of one identity (child, outsider) and transcendence into another, a presumed higher social identity (adult, insider).

In advertisements for bath products transcendence is promised. But the call is not to lose one's identity in service of a higher ideal. The transformation is not toward a new social identity but toward a nonsocial or even antisocial identity. Bath products speak of spirit and soul, but never of sacrifice, sin, or striving. Instead, advertisements encourage readers to seek pure pleasure in self-indulgence. They retreat from the world into fantasy but return essentially unchanged. Unlike rituals properly understood, the bath ritual here is asocial, as it leaves out a key element in the creation and re-creation of identity, namely, other people. In Morocco the women's bath is a communal place, a secret society where a woman can escape family burdens in the supportive company of other women. By contrast, the Western woman retreats not into the company of other women but into the privacy of her bathroom. As writer Margaret Laurence once remarked, "How strange to have to keep on retreating to the only existing privacy, the only place one is permitted to be unquestionably alone, the lavatory."[3] Advertisers, by contrast, do not find it strange at all:

> Vitabath can take your body and soul to the ultimate dimension of bathing.
> Bath-time is your time for daydreams and indulgence.
> The time to lose yourself in a beautiful private world . . .
> relaxing away the cares of a busy day or starting a new day refreshed and serene.

> Pour yourself a bath-full of Charlie bubbles.
> Step into the silky luxury of the pale-tinted water.
> Smooth and foam all over to cleanse your skin . . .
> It's a bath that's good to your body, great for your soul!

Despite the emphasis on losing oneself in dreams while preparing to affirm oneself in social reality, these private rituals are, in truth, little more than patterned behavior. They lack what anthropologist Victor Turner called the "multivocality of symbols," in which symbolic objects and movements call up the complexity of cultural and natural life. It is what it is, and little more. Rituals, by contrast, act economically, taking the complex and reducing it down to relatively simple steps in which one object—a cock, a color, a dance step, may signify many different cultural oppositions.[4] Within rituals, people reenact the dominant myths of their culture: the stories they tell themselves that resolve the tensions between these oppositions, and that help them as individuals and as a society through the moments of transition, as between the stages of a person's life, or the seasons of the year. One of the major transitions for women is that from biological girlhood to womanhood, as marked by the onset of menstruation.

Purity and Pollution

Menstrual blood once symbolized both pollution and power. It represented woman's ability to bring forth new life; some cultures did not credit men with having anything to do with procreation. Women's cycles were tied to the cycles of the moon, to the cycles of growth on earth. Because of her mysterious powers, the menstruating woman was held to be dangerous, and various taboos were respected concerning her. In *The Fear of Women* Wolfgang Lederer provides a short list:

> Zoroaster had menstruating women punished for approaching either fire or water; and a Hindu woman during her period must seclude herself . . . and her son must avoid her as a mysteriously dangerous, blood stained witch or demon. An Australian aborigine who discovered that his wife had lain on his blanket at her menstrual period, killed her and died of terror himself within a fortnight. Among the Bribri Indians of Costa Rica a menstruous woman may eat only from banana leaves, which, once she has done with them, she throws away in some sequestered spot; for were a cow to find them, and eat them, the animal would waste away and perish.[5]

To some, such taboos represent the oppression of women, to others, grudging recognition of their powers. Anthropologist Mary Douglas adopts a more balanced stance when she claims that such menstrual taboos, along with other taboos regarding pollution, represent one of the ways through which a society elaborates a culture and differentiates among its members. Thus "ideas about sexual dangers are better interpreted as symbols of the relations between parts of society . . . the two sexes can serve as a model for the collaboration and distinctiveness of social units."[6] The symbolic power of woman's menstrual flow develops out of the particular culture. In some, the Hasidic Jewish communities, for example, the sexual taboos associated with woman's period allow it to become a time of separation and renewal. Jeannette Kupfermann reports how one Hasidic woman referred to these taboos as a "hedge of roses," meaning "they were a beautiful way of keeping the marriage partnership fresh and alive."[7] Douglas goes so far as to suggest that there may be an inverse relationship between the presence of sexual taboos, indirect repression, if you will, and the level of sexual violence, or direct repression. "Sex is likely to be pollution-free in a society where sexual roles are enforced directly."[8] An interesting hypothesis, given the rising rate of sexual violence in our society, but one that must be explored elsewhere.

Thus the anthropological evidence suggests a powerful symbolic potentiality in women's periodicity. If one turns to contemporary advertisements for related products, however, the images are not of fecundity. They are of sterility. Science has demystified woman's biological power and supposedly secret knowledge, substituting in its place its own values and language. It has wiped the "curse" from view, freeing women to participate in the modern age. No danger, but also no power. No unpredictability, no menstrual "accidents." In tampon and pad advertisements, the mastery of science is represented by technological breakthroughs tested and proved through experimentation:

> Maxithins maxiabsorbent materials lock-in fluids
> better than the materials in maxi-pads.
> This blotter test proves it . . .
> 18 mls. fluid was poured on each pad.
> After blotting in as little as 10 minutes,
> the surface of the MAXITHINS was drier.

To avoid women's suffering the least discomfort, scientists turn their attention to problems of female anatomy and physiology, arriving at solutions that respect female delicacy. Playtex introduces its "unique 'Gentle Glide' applicator" to "make sure that insertion is easier and more comfortable from the very start." Once inserted, its tampons exhibit "unique blooming action. . . . They open up like a flower, and adapt to your natural body shape to help protect you against by-pass leakage and embarrassing staining . . . ." Finally, "more complete protection" is achieved through "deodorant confidence," providing that "extra reassurance."

Lingering cultural images of menstruation as pollution are cleared away by reference to how clean women will feel by using a given product, as in "now . . . maxi days are *cleaner* days." The model, dressed in white lingerie, looks out past the breezy white curtain at the bright white sunshine, with the white pads featured in the advertisement's foreground.

> Imagine the surface of a maxi-pad staying clean! Well, that's the idea behind our new StayClean Surface. Fluid passes through and gets buried within the pad. The surfaces actually stays cleaner, so you'll feel cleaner.
>
> All-new Stayfree Silhouette Maxi-pads. They're shaped to fit and designed to give you a cleaner kind of protection.

Again we see a quasi-sacred imagery. A sense of baptism, cleansing, and rebirth, with the light coming in from the upper-left corner to which the acolyte responds, the dawning of a new day. Purity and pollution imagery lingers, even if the pollution is controlled and denied.

Because she is like a small girl afraid to venture into the world, the adult woman is promised total safety. In contrast to the taboos of other societies, in ours the promise is that

absolutely no societal notice will be given to the menstruating
woman. Her menses must be invisible; when it becomes visible,
control has failed. She has had an "accident":

> If your maxi doesn't look like this,
> you could be having a few too many accidents.

> If you almost had an "accident" in the office last month,
> you're not alone . . .
> Sometimes I think my period knows when a really busy
> week is coming up . . . The week the boss gives me a
> special rush assignment. The week everything was
> needed yesterday . . . One day recently, I could have
> done without my period.
> The phones were ringing like crazy. A few packages and
> their messengers got lost. And there I was trying to type a
> report which had two hours to make the plane. I kept
> telling myself I ought to take a break, but something inside
> me said "5 more minutes." Then, all of a sudden, I
> remembered my period.
> I rushed down the hall to the ladies' room, expecting the
> worst. I'd had an accident, but only my panties and I knew.

This advertisement reinforces both a stereotyped image of the
woman at work, typing for her boss, and a stereotyped image of
the female mentality, worrisome and pettily conformist. It is
important that no one but the panties knew, not even the female
coworkers. Menstruation becomes a personal *problem* that must
be dealt with *individually*. Another advertisement curiously
contrasts remaining female social rituals with the lack of ritual
surrounding this biological fact. We see depicted six candid
snapshots of women enjoying themself at "Donna's shower. It
was a very special day":

Special days like a bridal shower, your first prom, graduation—those days have to be perfect. That's when you can trust Tampax . . . Tampax tampons . . . because special days should never be trusted to anything less.

In our society a girl fears not that she will not be singled out for special treatment, but rather that she will be noticed. She fears starting her periods relatively early or late in her teens. "Sheena, who's 13, started her periods quite early, when she was just eleven. As an early starter, she got embarrassed very easily about her periods." She fears that it will prevent her participation in peer group activities, that it will restrict her "fun." Two teenage girls bask on a sunny beach. Lisa, age fourteen, confides, "I would still be using pads if it weren't for Tampax tampons":

I still can't believe how long I put up with using pads. A week's vacation at the beach would've been ruined because of them. I went away with my best friend Jan and her folks. And wouldn't you know—that's when I get my period! Of course, there's no way I'd wear a bathing suit or shorts—with a pad. Too bulky! I told Jan how I felt and that's when I found out about Petal Soft Tampax tampons.

The main thing is that girls and women should not miss out on the fun. Any remaining awe associated with this visible sign of childbearing potentiality pales beside the new freedom afforded by modern sanitary products. And how is this freedom used? Besides the freedom of joining in leisure activities ("You can play tennis, dance, run, and swim . . ."), the associated freedom is that of being able to wear whatever you want. The blond in the spanking clean white shirt and pants set tells us,

"It's the heaviest day of my period, and I'm not wearing a
tampon or a thick pad. . . ." The copy reinforces the point:

> So, if you're looking to solve the problem of what to
> wear from day one, wear New Sure & Natural Maxishields
> and wear whatever you want.

As another product (o.b. tampons) says, "Keep it simple and set
yourself free." The lithe young woman in the striped bathing
suit reinforces British sociologist Judith Williamson's point that
the ideal female figure is a boyish figure.[9] All these advertisements similarly serve to deny adult biological womanhood,
its biological potentialities along with its adult responsibilities.
With period controlled and invisible, the woman is free to remain
a girl, to participate in the fun, to be just like one of the boys.

Rituals of Exchange

The slim model stretches snakelike across her couch in an
advertisement for watches. She asks the man, the salesman,
nobody in particular, "Is it so shameless . . . to be so sure of
something so expensive?"

> She'd said all along it had to be a watch by Audemars
> Piguet.
> She'd just smiled and said I'd better see one.
> In the quiet calm of an eminent jewelers the man
> selected a watch reverently from the suede-lined case.
> . . .
> As he held it out, the intricately woven bracelet snaked
> through his fingers like liquid gold . . .
> This was an expensive watch.
> Very. She lowered her eyes as he told her the price.

Almost hesitated. Then looked up at me inquiringly.
"Well?"
"No," I said softly.
"Certainly about something as beautiful as this one can
never be shameless. At any price."

The only shame would be if the man were to refuse to buy
the watch because of the price. For the gift represents a form of
excess, of spending, of redistribution. In some societies it was
structured into the practice of potlatch, whereby the wealthiest
or most powerful make a symbolic display of getting rid of
and/or redistributing their goods. Through the bestowal of a
gift, the giver is demonstrating his superior position in society
and also tying the receiver more closely to him. The woman in
the advertisement is at one and the same time rewarded and
indebted. Recognizing that she is a prize (and a prize for which
he is willing to pay), he now establishes the terms of the
relationship. The gift comes to represent the power contract,
his economic power in exchange for her sexual power. If it were
merely affection, gifts of equal value would be exchanged with
equal frequency between equally solvent partners. Such, traditionally, has not been the case. "I really think that American
gentlemen are the best after all, because . . . kissing your hand
may make you feel very, very good, but a diamond and sapphire
bracelet lasts forever."[10]
     Jewelry is presented as the measure of what a man is willing
to pay for a woman. It represents the reward for feminine
virtue, or for its surrender. Though jewelry advertisements
increasingly encourage women to buy expensive items for
themselves, expensive jewelry has traditionally been purchased
as a gift. It is usually a gift from the more powerful/rich to the
less powerful/rich: from men to women, parents to children, or
even a successful son to devoted mother. There are, of course,
exceptions, such as Father's Day cufflinks or a tie clasp, but

such exceptions make a small pile of trinkets compared to the bracelets, earrings, pins, and necklaces bestowed upon women, by men. In our society women are not supposed to be concerned about the price of gifts they receive. "Expensive yes, but I'm worth it."

The fundamental importance of this underlying exchange principle between women and jewels is reflected in advertisements that focus more on the giving than on the gift:

> He bought the cube [cube-shaped gold necklace] so I bought the round [of liquor].

Not exactly economic reciprocity. In a second advertisement the foreground features a man's hand dangling an expensive gold and diamond watch, while the background holds an inviting glass of champagne. The copy reads, "I'll show you a really special time tonight." Who could resist both champagne and a $4,500 watch?

On traditional days or key moments in a relationship, women are rewarded for being good daughters, lovers, or mothers. Or they may be rewarded for being not so good: as Mae West said, "When I'm bad, I'm better."

The first of these occasions, traditionally, is when the girl turns sixteen. Her rejection of tomboy freedoms and habits, her pubescent awkwardness, all is forgotten as she achieves this marker of status as a young woman which used to, and to some extent may still, signal her entrance into the marriage market. The girl is presented with a sweetheart necklace because she *is* a sweetheart, the first of many equations of women with their jewels. "Precious Sweethearts for only $24.95."

Soon, handsome dates will, theoretically, appear with such small rewards. In a "Gold is for Lovers" advertisement the teenage model fondles her dangling gold earrings and remarks, "And I've only known him a week." Scarlett O'Hara was taught that the only proper gifts an unattached woman could receive were handkerchiefs, but the modern belles in advertisements exhibit no such inhibitions. In fact, one grinning model playfully chewing on a diamond earring tells Scarlett to "go cry in your petticoat," while another pulls a diamond necklace playfully up across her face, announcing, "Gable, I'm ready."

But these are merely way-stations. The diamond ring symbolizes the transaction, the successful completion of the courtship.

Although the transition from girlhood into biological adulthood has become nearly invisible to society, that between the single state and marriage is still cause for much activity—and expense. Special magazines such as *Modern Bride* are packed with bridal gowns of the most traditional mode; like icons, these brides all appear as variations on one saintly theme. They will soon surround themselves with the honorific items of their station: silver, china, new mattresses, and major appliances.

The glamour magazines largely leave this specialized market to the brides' magazines (aside from annual special segments— because it is June, because they have to fill their editorial pages with something, whether old, new, or borrowed—but seldom blue). But they do regularly include advertisements for engagement and wedding rings. Such rings symbolize not simply individual commitment, but commitment to social adulthood, acceptance of the appropriate roles of wife and mother. It is seen as only fitting, then, that the ring should be as weighty, in terms of cost, carets, and significance, as the decision itself.

But young people performing this ritual exchange for the first time may understandably experience some confusion. Like young people in other cultures, then, they turn to those whom anthropologists label the *adepts*—select older people who are skilled in the ritual steps to be performed and in their significance. Authors of etiquette books, religious figures, and even mothers all contribute advice to the uninitiated, but in the

magazine advertisements the leading adepts are the jewelers.
These wise men (they are always shown as men) help the young
couple set off on the right path.

CONFUSED?

You had only to look inside your heart to know you'd
found the perfect love. But finding the perfect diamond
ring raises technical questions the heart can't answer.
Seems like you'd need the world's largest jeweler to clear
up the confusion.

Well, the world's largest jeweler is Zales . . .

The bride asks:

Is 2 months' salary too much to spend for something
that lasts forever?

She describes the problem:

Jim's a hopeless romantic. I'm the ultimate pragmatist.
So I was a little worried about his going overboard on my
diamond engagement ring.

Then again, I didn't want to discourage him too much.
So instead of telling him I didn't need a diamond, and
kicking myself later, I made sure he saw a jeweler just to
get some sort of spending guideline. And he found out that
today you can get a really nice diamond, without breaking
your budget, for about 2 months salary.

Jim says it's the best 2 months he's ever spent.

Four diamonds, ranging in price from $600 to $6,000, are
pictured below the photograph of the relieved young woman
embracing her Jim. The Diamond Information Center would
have their views become female cultural currency, leaving it up

to the women to manipulate the men. Another advertisement depicts two young female friends, presumably roommates at State U. (according to the triangular flag in the background), huddled on the edge of their dormitory beds and admiring the lucky one's engagement ring. "What a big, beautiful diamond," says the supportive friend, adding, "You're fiancé must be really rich!"

> Rich? No way. In fact, we didn't think we'd ever spend $1,200 on an engagement ring. We figured all the good ones would be way out of our price range, which we had originally set at $600. So of course we were nervous about going shopping for it.
>
> Well, the jeweler put us right at ease. He let us examine several different diamonds . . . And then he gave us a great tip on how much we should spend on the ring. He said that today, a diamond engagement ring should be worth at least one to two months salary . . .
>
> The ring we finally chose cost us several hundred more than we had planned. But I think it was worth every penny. After all, Jack gets as big a kick out of the compliments as I do.

As long as he's happy. Notice the mock reluctance of these two women, a disingenuousness displayed in another advertisement where a handsome young man strokes away the tears of joy from his fiancée's cheeks: "Could this be the girl who told me she didn't care about diamonds?" This reflects the stereotype that women say one thing, but mean another, which the man has to guess. Promise her anything, but give her a diamond. It is worth it. It lasts. It implies the marriage will, too.

> A return of white weddings.
> Lifelong love.

Wedding rings of Platinum
Because you want it to last

In the advertising text gifts should not necessarily stop coming after marriage. The husband should still "let her know romance is not a dead language." Away on business, he should think of her back home. "This trip, I had a little free time," meaning time enough to pick up the gold bracelet shown. "Give her a food processor. Or give her a present." The accompanying photograph shows a smiling husband bestowing a gold necklace on his wife, well aware that "nothing feels like giving real gold." Finally, De Beers encourages successful men not to forget the little woman who made it all possible: "Show the world you couldn't have made it without her."

Along with jewelry, the other traditional reward for female beauty and sexual compliance is fur. Perhaps more than any other product except the wedding ring, the fur coat symbolizes both the status of possession and the possession of status. In this dual process, women, as they don their minks, also assume the status of possession in both a sexual and financial sense. The wealthy man, aging and not always attractive, makes a grand entrance with his beautifully furred young female, thereby demonstrating that he owns her as he owns his Cadillac or Mercedes. He can afford her. Rightly or wrongly, he possesses status in other men's eyes through his apparent possession of her as an expensive and desirable object. As the woman cuddles in the fur's warm sensuality, she assumes a childlike dependency and deceptive security. Recall the popular image of the girl/woman discovering the hoped-for fur coat among the presents under the Christmas tree.

By giving a fur to a woman, the man performs the ultimate cultural gesture, one with echoes of primitive exchange and protection. While the wealthiest may ask for Swiss bank accounts, many women know they *should* dream of the fur as the ultimate experience and reward. When a young woman accepts a fur coat from an admirer, she signals her acceptance of dependent status. The possibility of her making a similarly expensive gift in return, given the disparity in income between the sexes, is rare indeed. When an older woman, a wife, wears a fur, it may symbolize more by way of her own possession of status, albeit closely tied to her husband's occupational status. By a certain age, the wife of a doctor or lawyer may feel that she has earned her mink as he has earned the Mercedes; it goes with the job. This sense of fair dues may be reinforced if by any chance she has chosen to "look the other way" on the occasion of any husbandly peccadilloes. In such a case, the fur coat assumes the form of payoff. Thus, the fur may symbolize the last desperate measure in a marriage, or the first major victory in a seduction.

A few advertisements are trying to even up the exchange, and increase profits further, by selling men and women on the idea of "the man's diamond." To the extent that women can afford to and actually do buy men expensive gifts, the gesture will be symbolic of their new financial empowerment. To begrudge the expense in ritual is to begrudge the whole idea. Rituals—whether they entail gift giving or festivities marking key transitions or both—are by their nature uneconomical, wasteful, and unproductive.[11]

They are also necessary, in some shape or form. Advertisements use the idea of rituals to reinforce attitudes regarding what we should celebrate in our society, including beauty and social approval, and what we should ignore as best as possible, including, as we have seen, certain facts of female biology. Thus nature, once again, here in the guise of biological womanhood, is at war with culture, in the form of carefully constructed gender appearances. Advertisements offer products that promise to help women manage the former, in order to maintain the latter.

ELEVEN
A Gentleman and a Consumer

There are no men's beauty and glamour magazines with circulations even approaching those of the women's magazines we have been examining here. The very idea of men's beauty magazines may strike one as odd. In our society men traditionally were supposed to make the right appearance, to be well groomed and neatly tailored. What they were *not* supposed to do was to be overly concerned with their appearance, much less vain about their beauty. That was to be effeminate, and not a "real man." Male beauty was associated with homosexuals, and "real men" had to show how red-blooded they were by maintaining a certain distance from fashion.

Perhaps the best-known male fashion magazine is *GQ* founded in 1957 and with a circulation of 446,000 in 1986. More recently, we have seen the launching of *YMF* and *Young Black Male,* which in 1987 still have few advertising pages. *M* magazine, founded in 1983, attracts an audience "a cut above" that of *GQ.*[1]

Esquire magazine, more venerable (founded in 1933), is

classified as a general interest magazine. Although it does attract many women readers, many of the columns and features and much of the advertising are definitely directed toward attracting the attention of the male readers, who still make up the overwhelming majority of the readership.

As mentioned in the introduction, the highest circulations for men's magazines are for magazines specializing either in sex (*Playboy,* circulation 4.1 million; *Penthouse,* circulation nearly 3.8 million; and *Hustler,* circulation 1.5 million) or sports (*Sports Illustrated,* circulation 2.7 million).[2] That these magazines share an emphasis on power—either power over women or over other men on the playing field—should not surprise. In fact, sociologist John Gagnon would argue that sex and sports now represent the major fields in which the male role, as defined by power, is played out, with physical power in work, and even in warfare, being less important than it was before industrialization and technological advance.[3]

If we are looking for comparative evidence as to how advertisements define gender roles for men and women, we should not then see the male role as defined primarily through beauty and fashion. This seems an obvious point, but it is important to emphasize how different cultural attitudes toward both the social person and the physical body shape the gender roles of men and women. These cultural attitudes are changing, and advertisements are helping to legitimate the use of beauty products and an interest in fashion for men, as we shall see. As advertisements directed toward women are beginning to use male imagery, so too advertisements for men occasionally use imagery resembling that found in advertisements directed toward women. We are speaking of two *modes,* then. As Baudrillard writes, these modes "do not result from the differentiated nature of the two sexes, but from the differential logic of the system. The relationship of the Masculine and the Feminine to real men and women is relatively arbitrary."[4]

Increasingly today, men and women use both modes. The two great terms of opposition (Masculine and Feminine) still, however, structure the forms that consumption takes; they provide identities for products and consumers.

Baudrillard agrees that the feminine model encourages a woman to please herself, to encourage a certain complacency and even narcissistic solicitude. But by pleasing herself, it is understood that she will also please others, and that she will be chosen. "She never enters into direct competition. . . . If she is beautiful, that is to say, if this woman is a woman, she will be chosen. If the man is a man, he will choose his woman as he would other objects/signs (HIS car, HIS woman, HIS eau de toilette)."[5]

Whereas the feminine model is based on passivity, complacency, and narcissism, the masculine model is based on exactingness and choice.

> All of masculine advertising insists on rule, on choice, in terms of rigor and inflexible minutiae. He does not neglect a detail . . . It is not a question of just letting things go, or of taking pleasure in something, but rather of distinguishing himself. To know how to choose, and not to fail at it, is here the equivalent of the military and puritanical virtues: intransigence, decision, "virtus."[6]

This masculine model, these masculine virtues, are best reflected in the many car advertisements. There, the keywords are masculine terms: *power, performance, precision.* Sometimes the car is a woman, responding to the touch and will of her male driver, after attracting him with her sexy body. "Pure shape, pure power, pure Z. It turns you on." But, as the juxtaposition of shape and power in this advertisement suggest, the car is not simply other; it is also an extension of the owner. As he turns it on, he turns himself on. Its power is his power; through it, he will be able to overpower other men and impress and seduce women.

> How well does it perform?
> How well can you drive? (Merkur XR4Ti)

> The 1987 Celica GT-S has the sweeping lines and aggressive stance that promise performance. And Celica keeps its word.

> Renault GTA:
> Zero to sixty to zero in 13.9 sec.
> It's the result of a performance philosophy where acceleration and braking are equally important.
> There's a new Renault sports sedan called GTA. Under its slick monochromatic skin is a road car with a total performance attitude. . . . It's our hot new pocket rocket.

In this last example, the car, like the driver, has a total performance attitude. That is what works. The slick monochromatic skin, like the Bond Street suit, makes a good first impression. But car, like owner, must have what it takes, must be able to go the distance faster and better than the competition. This point is explicitly made in advertisements in which the car becomes a means through which this masculine competition at work is extended in leisure. Some refer directly to the manly sport of auto-racing: "The Mitsubishi Starion ESI-R. Patiently crafted to ignite your imagination. Leaving little else to say except . . . gentlemen, start your engines." Others refer to competition in the business world: "To move ahead fast in this world, you've got to have connections. The totally new Corolla FX 16 GT-S has the right ones." Or in life in general. "It doesn't take any [Japanese characters] from anyone. It won't stand for any guff from 300ZX. Or RX-7. Introducing Conquest Tsi, the new turbo sport coupe designed and built by Mitsubishi in Japan." Or Ferrari, which says simply, "We are the competition." In this competition between products, the owners become almost superfluous. But the advertisements, of course, suggest that the qualities of the car will reflect the qualities of the owner, as opposed to the purely abstract, apersonal quality of money needed for purchase. Thus, like the would-be owner, the BMW also demonstrates a "relentless refusal to compromise." It is for "those who thrive on a maximum daily requirement of high performance." While the BMW has the business attitude of the old school ("aggression has never been expressed with such dignity"), a Beretta suggests what it takes to survive today in the shark-infested waters of Wall Street. In a glossy three-page cover foldout, a photograph of a shark's fin cutting through indigo waters is accompanied by the legend "Discover a new species from today's Chevrolet." The following two pages show a sleek black Beretta similarly cutting through water and, presumably, through the competition: "Not just a new car, but a new species . . . with a natural instinct for the road . . . Aggressive stance. And a bold tail lamp. See it on the road and you won't soon forget. Drive it, and you never will."

And as with men, so with cars. "Power corrupts. Absolute power corrupts absolutely" (Maserati). Not having the money to pay for a Maserati, to corrupt and be corrupted, is a source of embarrassment. Advertisements reassure the consumer that he need not lose face in this manly battle. Hyundai promises, "It's affordable. (But you'd never know it.)"

> On first impression, the new Hyundai Excel GLS Sedan might seem a trifle beyond most people's means. But that's entirely by design. Sleek European design, to be exact.

Many advertisements suggest sexual pleasure and escape, as in "Pure shape, pure power, pure Z. It turns you on." Or "The all-new Chrysler Le Baron. Beauty . . . with a passion for driving." The Le Baron may initially suggest a beautiful female, with its "image of arresting beauty" and its passion "to drive. And drive it does!" But it *is* "Le Baron," not "La Baronness." And the advertisement continues to emphasize how it *attacks* [emphasis mine] the road with a high torque, 2.5 fuel-injected engine. And its turbo option can blur the surface of any passing lane." Thus the object of the pleasure hardly has to be female if it is beautiful or sleek. The car is an extension of the male that conquers and tames the (female) road: "Positive-response suspension will calm the most demanding roads." The car becomes the ultimate lover when, like the Honda Prelude, it promises to combine power, "muscle," with finesse. Automobile advertisements thus play with androgyny and sexuality; the pleasure is in the union and confusion of form and movement, sex and speed. As in any sexual union, there is ultimately a merging of identities, rather than rigid maintenance of their separation. Polymorphous perverse? Perhaps. But it sells.

Though power, performance, precision as a complex of traits find their strongest emphasis in automobile advertisements, they also appear as selling points for products as diverse as shoes, stereos, and sunglasses. The car performs on the road, the driver performs for women, even in the parking lot, as Michelin suggests in its two-page spread showing a male from waist down resting on his car and chatting up a curvaceous female: "It performs great. And looks great. So, it not only stands out on the road. But in the parking lot. Which is one more place you're likely to discover how beautifully it can handle the curves" (!).

As media analyst Todd Gitlin points out, most of the drivers shown in advertisements are young white males, loners who become empowered by the car that makes possible their escape from the everyday. Gitlin stresses the advertisements' "emphasis on surface, the blankness of the protagonist; his striving toward self-sufficiency, to the point of displacement from the recognizable world."[7] Even the Chrysler advertisements that coopt Bruce Springsteen's "Born in the USA" for their "Born in America" campaign lose in the process the original political message, "ripping off Springsteen's angry anthem, smoothing it into a Chamber of Commerce ditty as shots of just plain productive-looking folks, black and white . . . whiz by in a montage-made community." As Gitlin comments, "None of Springsteen's losers need apply—or rather, if only they would roll up their sleeves and see what good company they're in, they wouldn't feel like losers any longer."[8]

This is a world of patriarchal order in which the individual male can and must challenge the father. He achieves identity by breaking loose of the structure and breaking free of the pack. In the process he recreates the order and reaffirms the myth of masculine independence. Above all, he demonstrates that he knows what he wants; he is critical, demanding, and free from the constraints of others. What he definitely does not want, and goes to some measure to avoid, is to appear less than masculine, in any way weak, frilly, feminine.

Avoiding the Feminine

Advertisers trying to develop male markets for products previously associated primarily with women must overcome the taboo that only women wear moisturizer, face cream, hair spray, or perfume. They do this by overt reference to masculine symbols, language, and imagery, and sometimes by confronting the problem head-on.

There is not so much of a problem in selling products to counteract balding—that traditionally has been recognized as a male problem (a bald woman is a sexual joke that is not particularly amusing to the elderly). But other hair products are another story, as the March 1987 *GQ* cover asks, "Are you man enough for mousse?" So the advertisements must make their products seem manly, as with S-Curl's "wave and curl kit" offering "The Manly Look" on its manly model dressed in business suit and carrying a hard hat (a nifty social class compromise), and as in college basketball sportscaster Al McGuire's testimonial for Consort hair spray:

> "Year's ago, if someone had said to me, 'Hey Al, do you use hair spray?' I would have said, 'No way, baby!' "
> "That was before I tried Consort Pump."
> "Consort adds extra control to my hair without looking stiff or phony. Control that lasts clean into overtime and post-game interviews . . ."
> Grooming Gear for Real Guys. *Consort.*

Besides such "grooming gear" as perms and hair sprays, Real Guys use "skin supplies" and "shaving resources." They adopt a "survival strategy" to fight balding, and the "Fila philosophy"—"products with a singular purpose: perform-ance"—for effective "bodycare." If they wear scent, it smells of anything *but* flowers: musk, woods, spices, citrus, and surf are all acceptable. And the names must be manly, whether symbol-izing physical power ("Brut") or financial power ("Giorgio VIP Special Reserve," "The Baron. A distinctive fragrance for men," "Halston—For the privileged few").

As power/precision/performance runs as a theme throughout advertising to men, so too do references to the business world. Cars, as we have seen, promise to share their owner's professional attitude and aggressive drive to beat out the competition. Other products similarly reflect the centrality of business competition to the male gender role. And at the center of this competition itself, the business suit.

> At the onset of your business day, you choose the suit or sportcoat that will position you front and center . . .
> The Right Suit can't guarantee he'll see it your way. The wrong suit could mean not seeing him at all.

Along with the Right Suit, the right shirt. "You want it every time you reach across the conference table, or trade on the floor, or just move about. You want a shirt that truly fits, that is long enough to stay put through the most active day, even for the taller gentleman." The businessman chooses the right cologne—Grey Flannel, or perhaps Quorum. He wears a Gucci "timepiece" as he conducts business on a cordless telephone from his poolside—or prefers the "dignity in styling" promised by Raymond Weil watches, "a beautiful way to dress for success."

Men's products connect status and success; the right products show that you have the right stuff, that you're one of them. In the 1950s C. Wright Mills described what it took to get ahead, to become part of the "power elite":

> The fit survive, and fitness means, not formal competence . . . but conformity with the criteria of those who have already succeeded. To be compatible with the top men is to act like them, to look like them, to think like them: to be of and for them—or at least to display oneself to them in such a way as to create that impression. This, in fact, is what is meant by "creating"—a well-chosen word—"a good impression." This is what is meant—and nothing else—by being a "sound man," as sound as a dollar. [9]

Today, having what it takes includes knowing "the difference between dressed, and well dressed" (Bally shoes). It is knowing that "what you carry says as much about you as what you put inside it" (Hartmann luggage). It is knowing enough to imitate Doug Fout, "member of one of the foremost equestrian families in the country."

> Because of our adherence to quality and the natural shoulder tradition, Southwick clothing was adopted by the Fout family years ago. Clearly, they have as much appreciation for good lines in a jacket as they do in a thoroughbred.

There it is, old money. There is no substitute for it, really, in business or in advertising, where appeals to tradition form one of the mainstays guaranteeing men that their choices are not overly fashionable or feminine, not working class or cheap, but, rather, correct, in good form, above criticism. If, when, they achieve this status of gentlemanly perfection, then, the advertisement suggests, they may be invited to join the club.

> When only the best of associations will do
>
> Recognizing style as the requisite for membership, discerning men prefer the natural shoulder styling of Racquet Club. Meticulously tailored in pure wool, each suit and sportcoat is the ultimate expression of the clubman's classic good taste.

Ralph Lauren has his Polo University Club, and Rolex picks up on the polo theme by sponsoring the Rolex Gold Cup held at the Palm Beach Polo and Country Club, where sixteen teams and sixty-four players competed for "the pure honor of winning, the true glory of victory":

It has added new lustre to a game so ancient, its history is lost in legend. Tamerlane is said to have been its patriarch. Darius's Persian cavalry, we're told, played it. It was the national sport of 16th-century India, Egypt, China, and Japan. The British rediscovered and named it in 1857.

The linking of polo and Rolex is uniquely appropriate. Both sponsor and sport personify rugged grace. Each is an arbiter of the art of timing.

In the spring of 1987, there was another interesting club event—or nonevent. The prestigious New York University Club was ordered to open its doors to women. This brought the expected protests about freedom of association—and of sanctuary. For that has been one of the points of the men's club. It wasn't open to women. Members knew women had their place, and everyone knew it was not there. In the advertisements, as in the world of reality, there is a place for women in men's lives, one that revolves around:

Sex and Seduction

As suggested earlier, the growing fascination with appearances, encouraged by advertising, has led to a "feminization" of culture. We are all put in the classic role of the female: manipulable, submissive, seeing ourselves as objects. This "feminization of sexuality" is clearly seen in men's advertisements, where many of the promises made to women are now made to men. If women's advertisements cry, "Buy (this product) and he will notice you," men's advertisements similarly promise that female attention will follow immediately upon purchase, or shortly thereafter. "They can't stay away from Mr.

J." "Master the Art of Attracting Attention." She says, "He's wearing my favorite Corbin again." Much as in the advertisements directed at women, the advertisements of men's products promise that they will do the talking for you. "For the look that says come closer." "All the French you'll ever need to know."

Although many advertisements show an admiring and/or dependent female, others depict women in a more active role. "I love him—but life in the fast lane starts at 6 A.M.," says the attractive blonde tying on her jogging shoes, with the "him" in question very handsome and very asleep on the bed in the background. (Does this mean he's in the slow lane?) In another, the man slouches silhouetted against a wall; the woman leans aggressively toward him. He: "Do you always serve Tia Maria . . . or am I special?" She: "Darling, if you weren't special . . . you wouldn't be here."

The masculine role of always being in charge is a tough one. The blunt new honesty about sexually transmitted diseases such as AIDS appears in men's magazines as in women's, in the same "I enjoy sex, but I'm not ready to die for it" condom advertisement. But this new fear is accompanied by old fears of sexual embarassement and/or rejection. The cartoon shows a man cringing with embarrassment in a pharmacy as the pharmacist yells out, "Hey, there's a guy here wants some information on Trojans." ("Most men would like to know more about Trojan brand condoms. But they're seriously afraid of suffering a spectacular and terminal attack of embarrassment right in the middle of a well-lighted drugstore.") Compared with such agony and responsibility, advertisements promising that women will *want* whatever is on offer, and will even meet the male halfway, must come as blessed relief. Men can finally relax, leaving the courting to the product and seduction to the beguiled woman, which, surely, must seem nice for a change.

Masculine Homilies

A homily is a short sermon, discourse, or informal lecture, often
on a moral topic and suggesting a course of conduct. Some of
the most intriguing advertisements offer just that, short state-
ments and bits of advice on what masculinity is and on how real
men should conduct themselves. As with many short sermons,
many of the advertising homilies have a self-congratulatory air
about them; after all, you do not want the consumer to feel bad
about himself.

What is it, then, to be a man? It is to be *independent.* "There
are some things a man will not relinquish." Among them, says
the advertisement, his Tretorn tennis shoes.

It is to *savor freedom.* "Dress easy, get away from it all and
let Tom Sawyer paint the fence," advises Alexander Julian, the
men's designer. "Because man was meant to fly, we gave him
wings" (even if only on his sunglasses).

It is to live a life of *adventure.* KL Homme cologne is "for the
man who lives on the edge." Prudential Life Insurance
preaches, "If you can dream it, you can do it." New Man
sportswear tells the reader, "Life is more adventurous when
you feel like a New Man."

It is to *keep one's cool.* "J. B. Scotch. A few individuals know
how to keep their heads, even when their necks are on the
line."

And it is to stay one step *ahead of the competition.* "Altec
Lansing. Hear what others only imagine." Alexander Julian
again: "Dress up a bit when you dress down. They'll think you
know something they don't."

What is it, then, to be a woman? It is to be *dependent.* " A
woman needs a man," reads the copy in the Rigolletto advertisement showing a young man changing a tire for a grateful
young woman.

The American cowboy as cultural model was not supposed to care for or about appearances. He was what he was, hard-working, straightforward, and honest. He was authentic. Men who cared "too much" about how they looked did not fit this model; the dandy was effete, a European invention, insufficient in masculinity and not red-blooded enough to be a real American. The other cultural model, imported from England, was the gentleman. A gentleman did care about his appearance, in the proper measure and manifestation, attention to tailoring and to quality, understatement rather than exaggeration.[10]

From the gray flannel suit of the 1950s to the "power look" of the 1980s, clothes made the man fit in with his company's image. Sex appeal and corporate correctness merged in a look that spelled success, that exuded confidence.

Whether or not a man presumed to care about his appearance, he did care about having "the right stuff," as Tom Wolfe and *Esquire* call it, or "men's toys," as in a recent special issue of *M* magazine. Cars, motorcycles, stereos, sports equipment: these are part of the masculine appearance. They allow the man to demonstrate his taste, his special knowledge, his affluence: to extend his control. He can be and is demanding, for only the best will do.

He also wants to be loved, but he does not want to appear needy. Advertisements suggest the magic ability of products ranging from cars to hair creams to attract female attention. With the right products a man can have it all, with no strings attached: no boring marital ties, hefty mortgages, corporate compromises.

According to sociologist Barbara Ehrenreich, *Playboy* magazine did much to legitimate this image of male freedom. The old male ethos, up to the postwar period, required exchanging bachelor irresponsibility for married responsibility, which also symbolized entrance into social adulthood.[11] The perennial bachelor, with his flashy cars and interchangeable women, was the object of both envy and derision; he had fun, but and because he was not fully grown up. There was something frivolous in his lack of purpose and application.

This old ethos has lost much of its legitimacy. Today's male can, as Baudrillard suggests, operate in both modes: the feminine mode of indulging oneself and being indulged and the masculine mode of exigency and competition. With the right look and the right stuff, he can feel confident and manly in boardroom or suburban backyard. Consumer society thus invites both men and women to live in a world of appearances and to devote ever more attention to them.

TWELVE
Conclusion

Putting on appearances is no simple matter. Becoming an object is not simply turning oneself into the "other" for another person, or for oneself. The beauty role is neither neat nor simple. Rather, it entails complex forms of cultural participation replete with psychological, social, and ritualistic significance. This is much of its appeal. This is why, in some measure, we will continue to be "inauthentic," why we will continue to live amid culture's complexities and contradictions, and not in some hypothetical state of nature where we can "just be ourselves." This is why we will continue to put on appearances.

This is not to say, however, that we shall, or must, continue to do so in the fashion advocated by advertisements. As we have seen, their content changes in response to other social changes. Debates about advertising raise broader questions about consumer society, its values, its social forms, its restrictions, and potentialities. Thus Stephen Fox is justified in saying that, although one may accuse American culture of being hedonistic, money-mad, and superficial, "to blame advertising for these most basic tendencies in American history is to miss the point":

> It is too obvious, too easy, a matter of killing the messenger instead of dealing with the bad news. The people who have created modern advertising are not hidden persuaders pushing our buttons in the service of some malevolent purpose. They are just producing an especially visible manifestation, good and bad, of the American way of life.[1]

As we emphasize the extent to which advertising reinforces these values and elaborates upon these cultural tendencies, we must realize that our concern with the shape of advertising is, in some measure, a concern over the shape of our society, over the content of our lives.

The most valid criticism of advertising is not that related to any particular abuse. There are informal and formal means to challenge specific advertisements that overstep community definitions of good taste and honesty, that either offend or mislead. The most valid criticism is, rather, that advertising taken as a whole comprises a "privileged discourse."[2] What is wrong is not its presence, but rather the increasingly felt absence of any competing set of cultural messages and values.

Advertising is part of our cultural surround. It sells products to preschoolers and to the elderly. It helps pay for the mass media to which we devote so much attention. Children now spend more time watching television than they do in school. Surely it is worth asking, what are they learning?

Sometimes goods promise that they will improve some identifiable part of our lives: mascara will not run down our cheeks, briefcases will organize our papers. Sometimes they promise so much more: mascara will make us loved, briefcases will bring success. Thus Michael Schudson is right in calling advertising "capitalist realism," interesting not so much for what it says about any one product as for what it says about our economic system and our society as a whole.[3]

Advertising as capitalist realism promises us that money, spent on goods, buys happiness. We come to accept this promise, consciously or unconsciously. We come to accept it as "natural" when advertising's discourse remains unchallenged by any other. We even accept that money can buy us distinction, can provide for us that appearance of being unique, of standing apart from the hoi polloi. So much advertising to women promises that the product will make the woman unique, will make her unforgettable: "Your Wind Song stays on his mind." However, as Simmel rightly recognized, distinction is that which is totally *other than,* different from, money. Money is a common standard that reduces differences, by which varied objects are reduced to one quantitative scale. True distinction, for Simmel, remains something apart, something truly unique to the individual, something that can never be translated into dollars and cents, something that can never be bought and sold.[4]

Advertisements thus promise to provide us with beauty, with happiness, with unique and instantaneous identities. They promise their own form of transcendence, a promise earlier made by religion and art. They promise that "suddenly, nothing will be the same." They also promise power and control, power over others, control of our own bodies and destinies.

It is no wonder that advertising stresses the appearance of youth and the values of youth. It is caught up with youth's crises and concerns, namely, finding identity and managing intimacy. It is about making *it* and about making *love,* both ambitions to be accomplished with the aid of strategic purchasing.

What it is *not* about are what have been identified by social psychologist Erik Erikson as the developmental tasks of adulthood, the mature person's developing sense of the importance of giving something back to community and society.[5] The social motive, an appreciation of the social good, rarely appears in advertising such as has been examined here. The magic word is the isolated *I*, not the connected *We*; the magic slogan is provided by L'Oréal: "This I do for me."

Thus, it is not so much a question of what advertising does as what it does not do. It affirms one set of values, coopting all others to serve its purpose, which is, of course, to sell products. Sometimes it serves to communicate nonprofit causes, such as the recent nationwide campaign against drug abuse. Worthy as this is, it should serve to underline the main object of advertising: to increase sales. As seen in this analysis, the advertising creative staff is adept at using whatever cultural and symbolic forms will serve this overriding purpose. Whatever reforms are suggested, advertising will still, must still, serve this end, a point that has been demonstrated even in socialist societies.[6]

Despite its position as a privileged discourse, advertising often comes to its own defense. Even among the "Me generation" there lingers some suspicion of a doubt that self-indulgence and self-actualization may not exhaust life's potential. The Protestant Ethic may be dead or dying, and duty now an empty word, someone else's "trip." A spirit of self-sacrifice, or even community service, may be increasingly foreign to us. But, as Baudrillard suggests, enough may remain enough of this social ethic to form implicit criticism of the narcissism and passivity, the search for love and status encouraged by conseumerism in general and advertising in particular. Advertising responds by contrasting the violence and deprivations of the world of events to the realm of beauty and security it creates. Our sense of having made the right choices in living in a material world is reaffirmed by reminders of the risks and dangers that exist outside its comforts and reassurances. As Baudrillard writes, "Consumer society sees itself as a Jerusalem that is encircled, rich but threatened; this is its ideology."[7]

Why else would advertising insist so hard that we have the right to enjoy ourselves, whether with a new car or a new hair color, that we deserve it, that we have earned it, even if it is just by being ourselves? It is fundamentally a question of value; there is still something at the heart of consumer society that does not make us sleep easy. Consider the full-page advertisement for *Cosmopolitan* that appeared in the *New York Times* on July 13, 1982. The attractive young woman in the plunging décolletage had the answer to our question of values. She asked, rhetorically:

"How do you rationalize loving Judith Leiber hand bags and Ralph Lauren hacking jackets with also loving humanity? Well, eschewing beautiful possessions doesn't make you a Certified Superior Person, and *liking* them doesn't make you shallow or selfish. My favorite magazine says care . . . be generous . . . write checks for people who need you to but don't get the guilts about the checks you write for *you*. You earned the *money*! I love that magazine. I guess you could say I'm that COSMOPOLITAN girl.

Surely it is not any attack from academia or the intelligentsia that might make advertisers sleep less easy. Such discourse as exists, even when it deconstructs images and appeals, reinforces the privileged position of advertising as discourse. Baudrillard again is on the mark when he writes,

Like all great myths, that of "consumer society" has its discourse and its anti-discourse; that is to say, that the exalted discourse of abundance finds its double in the "critical" counter-discourse, morose and moralising, on the misdeeds of consumer society and the tragic outcome that it can only have for all of civilisation.[8]

Behind the object lies the emptiness of human social relations, an emptiness created in large measure by the assembled forces of production, by the success of the capitalist experiment. What, then, is the alternative?

We could, as Catholic social thinker Ernest Renan suggested of other topics, simply stop talking about it. We could turn toward a more worthy topic, a revaluation of the intellectually devalued realms of religion, education, and art. This is now occurring, if this discourse is still only faintly heard.[9] But the "we" thus understood may be the intellectual few, whereas one of the goals of the critique of advertising was to have a broader impact on society, to reach the many, if not the mass.

Fortunately, this is not an either–or choice. We can *both* critique advertising as one cultural form and provide other forms, which, in creating a different language, provide a more forceful critique by the mere fact of suggesting alternatives. Jürgen Habermas has written of the need to establish "communicative rationality," and also of how culture and history can be made to serve progressive purposes and ends. Though he does not see this as an easy task, he does present it as one possibility, one means by which Baudrillard's emptiness of social relations could be replaced by a society with greater depth and human variety.[10]

It is not, then, a question of advertising per se but of the position of privilege we have allowed it, our own cultural and social passivity in letting it stand in place of so much more, of letting it do "the talking for us."

What it is also is a question of emphasis and proportion. As philosopher Janet Radcliffe-Richards writes of feminine attractiveness, "There really is a world of difference between deciding you must reluctantly stop putting so much effort into something which has been given too high a priority by tradition and treating that thing as something inherently *pernicious,* to be got rid of whether it is any trouble or not."[11]

It is not for me to give women, or men, their marching orders. It has been my task to examine the cultural content of advertising, to see how deeply rooted it is in our society and culture, how objectification is not an isolated "woman's problem" but a social fact for all, and part and parcel of consumer society. I have suggested that, if there is a problem with putting on appearances, it lies not simply in what advertising tells us to do, but with what it does not tell us to do, because that is not part of its job. I, for one, see advertising not simply as the shaper of men and women, but as shaped by men and women, the advertisers and the public. Let us work upon the hope that we can exercise the option of making our realities live up to, perhaps even exceed, our appearances.

Appendix

Women's Magazines

Category	Cosmo-politan	Essence	Glamour	Self	Seven-teen	Vogue
Clothing[a]	147	25	206	71	144	444
Scent[b]	72	21	56	30	41	70
Makeup[c]	222	49	195	122	117	180
Hair[d]	68	82	77	47	73	59
Reproduction[e]	51	11	39	31	26	9
Other health and body care[f]	61	11	20	22	19	13
Food[g]	36	35	42	47	10	17
Alcohol[h]	20	23	7	6	0	10
Cigarettes	57	32	43	29	0	35
Cars[i]	23	17	24	18	0	9
Travel[j]	3	20	10	2	0	11
Entertainment[k]	12	1	4	1	11	0
Equipment[l]	7	0	3	3	1	3
Books and magazines	17	3	20	8	7	14
Catalogues	21	3	14	3	1	14
Careers and education	2	8	7	2	10	0
Household[m]	26	4	14	0	8	15
Financial services[n]	3	5	5	4	0	8
Company image	0	23	0	0	6	0
Charity/public service	3	3	5	1	0	1
Products for opposite sex	17	2	3	2	0	11
Mixed category	4	1	2	0	4	5
Other	7	7	9	5	3	7
Total	879	386	805	454	481	935

Men's Magazines

Category	Esquire	Gentlemen's Quarterly	M
Clothing[a]	99	273	137
Scent[b]	25	35	12
Makeup[c]	4	14	2
Hair[d]	8	14	3
Reproduction[e]	0	1	0
Other health and body care[f]	1	3	0
Food[g]	16	7	0
Alcohol[h]	28	60	10
Cigarettes	11	10	0
Cars[i]	44	26	11
Travel[j]	23	7	0
Entertainment[k]	8	3	0
Equipment[l]	16	28	1
Books and magazines	1	7	2
Catalogues	1	1	1
Careers and education	0	3	0
Household[m]	9	7	0
Financial services[n]	12	3	3
Company image	1	1	0
Charity/public service	4	0	0
Products for opposite sex	2	3	3
Mixed category	2	1	2
Other	8	4	4
Total	323	511	191

Source: Advertisements in six women's magazines were coded for a six-month period, and in three men's magazines for a four-month period. All advertisements of at least half-page size were counted, and multipage advertisements of one product were counted as one advertisement.

[a] Includes lingerie, shoes, accessories, eyeglasses and sunglasses, and nylons and socks.

[b] Includes bath products, body sprays, and deodorants.

[c] Includes skin care products, foundations, powders, products for "eyes, lips, cheeks, and nails," and tanning products.

[d] Includes sprays, shampoos, relaxers, perms, accessories, and products for removal.

[e] Includes sanitary products, ovulation and pregnancy tests, and contraceptives.

[f] Includes exercise and fitness products, painkillers, dental products, non-food diet aids, and stimulants.

[g] Includes non-alcoholic drinks.

[h] Includes mixed drinks.

[i] Includes motorbikes, trucks, and tires.

[j] Includes spas and resorts, rent-a-car services, and luggage.

[k] Includes tapes, records, video, TVs, and movies.

[l] Includes car stereos and radar detectors and sporting equipment.

[m] Includes collectibles, accessories, china and silver, furniture, and cleaning products.

[n] Includes banks, cards, and insurance.

Notes

Introduction

1. Susan Bloch, "The Business of Friendly Persuasion," in *Duke Magazine* 71, No. 4 (March–April 1985): 12.
2. Karl Marx, "The Fetishism of Commodities," in Paul Connerton, ed., *Critical Sociology: Selected Readings* (Harmondsworth, England: Penguin, 1976), p. 75.
3. Georg Simmel, *The Philosophy of Money,* trans. Tom Bottomore and David Frisby (London: Routledge & Kegan Paul, 1978), p. 321.
4. Fernand Braudel, *The Structures of Everyday Life,* vol. 1, *Civilization and Capitalism 15th–18th Century,* trans. Sian Reynolds (New York: Harper & Row, 1979).
5. Charles Horton Cooley, *Life and the Student: Roadside Notes on Human Nature, Society, and Letters* (New York: Alfred A. Knopf, 1927), p. 200.
6. Francesco Alberoni, *Falling in Love,* trans. Lawrence Venuti (New York: Random House, 1984).

7. In David Frisby, *Fragments of Modernity: Theories of Modernity in the Work of Simmel, Kracauer and Benjamin* (Cambridge: MIT Press, 1986), pp. 18–19.

8. Richard Sennett, *The Fall of Public Man: On the Social Psychology of Capitalism* (New York: Vintage, 1974).

9. Christopher Lasch, *The Culture of Narcissism: American Life in an Age of Diminishing Expectations* (New York: Warner Books, 1979).

10. Alex Inkeles, *Exploring Individual Modernity* (New York: Columbia University Press, 1983), p. 315.

11. Michael Schudson, *Advertising, The Uneasy Persuasion: Its Dubious Impact on American Society* (New York: Basic Books, 1984).

12. The reference is, of course, to C. Wright Mills, *The Sociological Imagination* (New York: Oxford University Press, 1959).

13. Roland Marchand, *Advertising the American Dream: Making Way for Modernity, 1920–1940* (Berkeley: University of California Press, 1985), pp. 32–68 passim.

14. David Ogilvy, *Confessions of an Advertising Man* (New York: Atheneum, 1966), p. 96.

15. Thorstein Veblen, *The Theory of the Leisure Class: An Economic Study of Institutions* (New York: B. W. Huebsch, 1919).

16. E. S. Turner, *The Shocking History of Advertising!* (London: Michael Joseph, 1952), p. 213.

17. Jean Baudrillard, *La Société de consommation: Ses mythes, ses structures* (Paris: S.G.P.P., 1970), p. 213.

18. John Berger, *Ways of Seeing* (London: British Broadcasting Co., 1972), pp. 45–46.

19. Pamela L. Alreck, Robert E. Settle, and Michael A. Belch, "Who Responds to 'Gendered' Ads and How?" *Journal of Advertising Research* 22, No. 2 (April–May 1982): 25–32.

20. On the home, see Witold Rybcznski, *Home: A Short History of an Idea* (New York: Viking, 1986): Mihaly Csikszentmihalyi and Eugene Rochberg-Halton, *The Meaning of Things: Domestic Symbols and the Self* (Cambridge: Cambridge University

Press, 1981): and Gaye Tuchman, Arlene Kaplan Daniels, and James Benet, eds., *Hearth and Home: Images of Women in the Mass Media* (New York: Oxford University Press, 1978).

21. Simone de Beauvoir, *The Second Sex,* trans. H. M. Parshley (London: A Four Square Book, 1960), p. 29.

22. Susan Brownmiller, *Femininity* (New York: Simon & Schuster, 1984), p. 14.

23. Elaine Hatfield and Susan Sprecher, *Mirror Mirror . . . : The Importance of Looks in Everyday Life* (Albany: State University of New York Press, 1986).

24. Ibid. See also Glenn H. Elder, Jr., "Appearance and Education in Marriage Mobility," *American Sociological Review* 34 (1969): 519–33.

25. Georgia Dullea, "On Corporate Ladder, Beauty Can Hurt," *New York Times,* June 3, 1985, p. C13. See also Hatfield and Sprecher, *Mirror Mirror.*

26. Linda Wells, "The Bloom of Youth," *New York Times Magazine,* May 5, 1987, p. 86; *New York Times*, April 2, 1987, p. C2.

27. Irma Kurtz, *Malespeak* (London: Jonathan Cape, 1986), p. 80.

28. Rita Freedman, *Beauty Bound* (Lexington, Mass.: Lexington Books, 1985), p. x.

29. Nicholas D. Kristof, "Politics and the Art of Looking Good," *New York Times,* April 11, 1987, p. 4.

30. "Thoreau Out the First Ball, Bart," *Gentleman's Quarterly,* April 1987, pp. 67, 70.

31. Schudson, *Uneasy Persuasion.*

Madison Avenue: Method and Madness

1. See Daniel Pope, *The Making of Modern Advertising* (New York: Basic Books, 1983); Stephen Fox, *The Mirror Makers: A History of American Advertising and Its Creators* (New York: William Morrow, 1984); Schudson, *The Uneasy Persuasion;*

Marchand, *American Dream;* Ronald Berman, *Advertising and Social Control* (Beverly Hills, Calif.: Sage Publications, 1981); Erving Goffman, *Gender Advertisements* (London: Macmillan, 1976); Richard Wightman Fox and T. J. Jackson Lears, eds., *The Culture of Consumption: Critical Essays in American History, 1880–1980* (New York: Pantheon, 1983); Warren I. Susman, *Culture as History: The Transformation of American Society in the Twentieth Century* (New York: Pantheon, 1984); and Daniel J. Boorstin, *Image: A Guide to Pseudo-Events in America* (New York: Antheneum, 1962).

2. Neil McKendrick, John Brewer, and J. H. Plumb, *The Birth of Consumer Society: The Commercialization of Eighteenth Century England* (Bloomington: Indiana University Press, 1982).

3. Turner, *Shocking History of Advertising,* p. 25.

4. Lois Banner, *American Beauty* (New York: Alfred A. Knopf, 1983). See also Quentin Bell, *On Human Finery* (New York: Schocken, 1976); Alison Lurie, *The Language of Clothes* (New York: Random House, 1981); Valerie Steele, *Fashion and Eroticism: Ideals of Feminine Beauty from the Victorian Through the Jazz Age* (New York: Oxford University Press, 1985); Anne Hollander, *Seeing Through Clothes* (New York: Viking Press, 1980); and Elizabeth Wilson, *Adorned in Dreams: Fashion and Modernity* (London: Virago, 1985).

5. Rosalind Williams, *Dream Worlds* (Berkeley: University of California Press, 1982); and Gunther Barth, *City People: The Culture of the Modern City in Nineteenth-Century America* (New York: Oxford University Press, 1980). See also Susan Porter Benson, *Counter Cultures: Saleswomen, Managers and Customers in American Department Stores, 1890–1940* (Urbana: University of Illinois Press, 1986).

6. Marchand, *American Dream* pp. 25–69, passim.

7. James R. Adams, *Sparks Off My Anvil: From Thirty Years in Advertising* (New York: Harper & Bros. 1958), p. 37.

8. John Straiton, *Of Women and Advertising* (Toronto: McClelland and Stewart, 1984), p. 10.

9. Fox and Lears, *Culture of Consumption.* On character and personality, see also Ellen K. Rothman, *Hands and Hearts: A History of Courtship in America* (New York: Basic Books, 1984).

10. Bloch, "The Business of Friendly Persuasion," p. 12.

11. Stuart Ewen, *Captains of Consciousness: Advertising and the Social Roots of Consumer Culture* (New York: McGraw-Hill, 1976.

12. Schudson, *Uneasy Persuasion,* pp. 175–76.

13. Wilson B. Key, *Subliminal Seduction* (New York: New American Library, 1974).

14. Lucy Hughes Hallet, "Why Perfume Ads Stink," *Guardian,* April 1, 1986, p. 17.

15. Philip H. Dougherty, "Cold Water at Florida Gathering," *New York Times* March 27, 1987, p. D14. Dougherty does not provide separate comprehension levels for editorial material and advertisements. He does say that, although these levels were similar, advertisements because of their pictorial content were more likely to be understood.

16. Bostock, in Bloch, *Business of Friendly Persuasion.* p. 16.

17. David Ogilvy, *Confessions,* p. 150.

18. Adams, *Sparks,* p. 169.

19. Ibid.

20. Ibid., p. 158.

21. Edward Buxton, *Promise Them Anything: The Inside Story of the Madison Avenue Power Struggle* (New York: Stein & Day, 1972), p. 210.

22. Ibid.

23. Ogilvy, *Confessions,* p. 159.

24. Straiton, *Women and Advertising,* p. 156.

25. Buxton, *Promise Them Anything,* p. 51.

26. *New York Times,* December 14, 1986, sect. 6, p. 59.

27. Ogilvy, *Confessions,* p. 100.

28. William Leiss, Stephen Kline, and Sut Jhally, *Social Commu-*

nication in Advertising: Persons, Products, and Images of Well-Being (New York: Methuen, 1986), p. 34.

29. Ogilvy, *Confessions*, p. 20.
30. As Adams wrote, "Life is grist for the creative advertising man, just as it is for the writer of fiction. Wherever he goes and whatever he does, he should keep his eyes and ears open, and paper and pencil as close by as possible" (*Sparks*, p. 49).
31. Straiton, *Women and Advertising*, p. 40.
32. Arthur Koestler, *The Act of Creation* (New York: Macmillan, 1964).
33. John Berger, *Ways of Seeing* (London: British Broadcasting Co., 1972), p. 139.
34. Sara Rimer, "Odes to Jell-O: The Bards of Madison Avenue," *New York Times*, April 28, 1987, pp. B1–2.
35. Jessie Bernard, *The Female World* (New York: The Free Press, 1981).
36. For another examination of the limits and advantages of content analysis as interpretative analysis, see Jorge Arditi, "Content Analysis and Textual Interpretation," paper presented at the annual meeting of the Eastern Sociological Society, May 1–3, 1987, Boston.
37. Arthur Asa Berger, *Media Analysis Techniques* (Beverly Hills, Calif.: Sage Publications, 1982), p. 35.
38. Jean Baudrillard, "The Ecstasy of Communication," in Hal Foster, ed., *Post-Modern Culture* (London: Pluto Press, 1983), p. 126.
39. Georges Bataille, *Visions of Excess: Selected Writings, 1927–1939*, ed. Allan Stoekl, trans. Allan Stoekl with Carl R. Lovitt and Donald M. Leslie, Jr. (Manchester, England: Manchester University Press, 1985).
40. See for example Alice Embree, "Media Images 1: Madison Avenue Brainwashing—The Facts," in Robin Morgan, ed. *Sisterhood is Powerful: An Anthology of Writings from the Women's Liberation Movement* (New York: Random House, 1970), pp. 175–90; Janice Winship, "Advertising in Women's

Magazines: 1956–1974," occasional paper, Women's Series 59, Centre for Contemporary Cultural Studies, University of Birmingham, England, 1980; Gaye Tuchman, Arlene Kaplan Daniels, and James Benet, eds., *Hearth and Home: Images of Women in the Mass Media* (New York: Oxford University Press, 1978). For historical insight on women's homemaker role, see Ruth Schwartz Cowan, *More Work for Mother: The Ironies of Household from the Open Hearth to the Microwave* (New York: Basic Books, 1983).

41. See, among others, Susan Brownmiller, *Femininity* (New York: Simon & Schuster, 1984); Freedman, *Beauty Bound;* Robin Lakoff and Raquel Scherr, *Face Value: The Politics of Beauty* (London: Routledge & Kegan Paul, 1984). See also Kim Chernin, *The Obsession: Reflections on the Tyranny of Slenderness* (New York: Harper & Row, 1981) and *The Hungry Self: Daughters and Mothers, Eating and Identity* (New York: Times Books, 1985).

42. Connie Miller on women's magazines, in Bill Katz and Linda Sternberg Katz, *Magazines for Libraries,* 5th ed. (New York: R. R. Bowker, 1986), p. 993.

43. Ibid., p. 990.

44. Ibid., p. 992.

45. *Advertising Age,* February 16, 1987, p. 34.

46. Miller, in Katz and Katz, *Magazines,* p. 989.

47. Ibid.

48. Ibid., p. 933.

49. Edmund F. Santa Vicca on men's magazines, in Katz and Katz, *Magazines,* pp. 703–5.

50. Walter Benjamin commenting on Baudelaire, cited by Christine Buci-Glucksmann, "Catastrophic Utopia: The Feminine as Allegory of the Modern," in Catherine Gallagher and Thomas Laqueur, eds., *The Making of the Modern Body: Sexuality and Society in the Nineteenth Century* (Berkeley: University of California Press, 1987).

The Voices of Authority

1. Roland Barthes, *The Fashion System,* trans. Matthew Ward and Richard Howard (New York: Hill & Wang, 1983).
2. "Will a user at age 6 carry through?" asks the president of Revlon Beauty Group, U.S. See Linda Wells, "The Bloom of Youth," *New York Times Magazine,* May 5, 1987, p. 86.
3. One thinks of Carol Gilligan's discussion of the two different modes of moral thinking: *In a Different Voice: Psychological Theory and Women's Development* (Cambridge: Harvard University Press, 1982).
4. Pat Sloan, "Alfin Skin Line Ignites Controversy," *Advertising Age,* February 23, 1987, p. 32. See also William R. Greer, "F.D.A. Disputes Anti-Aging Cream Claims," *New York Times,* May 9, 1987, p. 56.
5. Hatfield and Sprecher, *Mirror Mirror,* p. 288. See also Jane Porcino, *Growing Older, Getting Better: A Handbook for Women in the Second Half of Life* (Reading, Mass.: Addison-Wesley, 1983).
6. Philip H. Dougherty, "Celebrity Brokers: A Busy Time," *New York Times,* March 2, 1987, p. D9.
7. Claude Atkin and Martin Block, "Effectiveness of Celebrity Endorsers," *Journal of Advertising Research* 23 (February–March 1983): 57–61.
8. Marchand, *American Dream,* p. 98.
9. Laurie Werner, "Megabuck Celebrities in the Halls of Commerce," *Cosmopolitan,* February 1987, p. 198.
10. Jeannette Kupfermann, *The MsTaken Body: A Fresh Perspective on the Women's Movement* (London: Granada, 1979), p. 43.
11. Mark Salmon, "Beauty as Elite Stigma: Notes on an Ambivalent Identity," paper presented at the annual meeting of the American Sociological Association, September 1983, Detroit.
12. Peter Carlson, "Swept Away By Her Sadness," *People,* October 24, 1983, pp. 34–37.

The Self Observed

1. In Tania Modleski, *Loving With a Vengeance: Mass-Produced Fantasies For Women* (New York: Methuen, 1982).
2. Rothman, *Hands and Hearts.*
3. Ibid.
4. Modleski, *Loving with a Vengeance.*
5. Simone de Beauvoir, *The Second Sex* (New York: Random House, 1952), p. 70.
6. Walter Benjamin, "The Work of Art in the Age of Mechanical Reproduction," in *Illuminations,* ed. Hannah Arendt, trans. Harry Zohn (New York: Schocken, 1969), pp. 217–51. See also Susan Sontag, *On Photography* (New York: Farrar, Straus & Giroux, 1977).
7. Jill Tweedie, *In The Name of Love* (New York: Patheon, 1979).
8. Modleski, *Loving With a Vengeance,* p. 34.
9. Ibid, p. 17.
10. Jean Baudrillard, *De la Séduction* (Paris: Editions Galilée, 1979), pp. 107–14.
11. Sigmund Freud, *Civilization and Its Discontents,* trans. James Strachey (New York: W. W. Norton, 1961).

Sex and Romance

1. Roland Barthes, *The Pleasure of the Text,* trans. Richard Miller (New York: Hill & Wang, 1975). See also Northrop Frye, *The Secular Scripture: A Study of the Structure of Romance* (Cambridge: Harvard University Press, 1976).
2. John Ruskin, "Sesame and Lilies," ed. Charles W. Eliot, *The Harvard Classics,* vol. 28 (New York: P. F. Collier & Son, 1910), pp. 95–170.
3. Bataille, *Visions of Excess,* pp. 10–14.
4. Barthes, *The Fashion System.*
5. Mary Wollstonecraft, *A Vindication of the Rights of Woman,*

ed. Carol H. Poston, Critical Edition Series (New York: Norton, 1976).

6. For several points of view on "The New Sobriety," see articles collected in the *Utne Reader* 21 (May–June 1987).

7. See Judith L. Laws and Pepper Schwartz, *Sexual Scripts* (Lanham, Md.: University Press of America, 1982). See also John H. Gagnon and Cathy S. Greenblatt, *Life Designs* (New York: Random House, 1977).

Beauty Status / Social Status

1. Thorstein Veblen, *The Theory of the Leisure Class: An Economic Study of Institutions* (New York: B. W. Huebsch, 1919).

2. Mary Douglas and Baron Isherwood, *The World of Goods* (New York: Basic Books, 1979).

3. See Georg Simmel, "The Metropolis and Mental Life," ed. Richard Sennett, *Classic Essays on the Culture of Cities* (New York: Prentice-Hall, 1969).

4. Berger, *Ways of Seeing,* pp. 132–33.

5. Ibid.

6. Georg Simmel, *The Philosophy of Money,* trans. Tom Bottomore and David Frisby (London: Routledge & Kegan Paul, 1978).

7. Ibid.

8. Veblen, *Leisure Class,* pp. 68–73.

9. Quentin Bell, *On Human Finery* (New York: Schocken, 1976).

The Geography of Beauty

1. See also the discussion in Barthes, *The Fashion System.*

2. Berger, *Ways of Seeing,* p. 133.

3. Marchand, *American Dream,* pp. 77–80.

4. Liza Crihfield Dalby, *Geisha* (Berkeley: University of California Press, 1983).

5. Shirley Abbott, *Womenfolks: Growing Up Down South* (New Haven: Ticknor & Fields, 1983), and Anne Firor Scott, *The Southern Lady: From Pedestal to Politics, 1830—1930* (Chicago: University of Chicago Press, 1970).

6. Banner, *American Beauty*, p. 11.

7. Berger, *Ways of Seeing*, pp. 146–49.

8. Ivan Illich, *Gender* (New York: Pantheon, 1982).

9. Bruno Bettelheim, *The Uses of Enchantment: The Meaning and Importance of Fairy Tales* (New York: Alfred A. Knopf, 1976).

10. See Beatrice Faust, *Women, Sex and Pornography: A Controversial and Unique Study* (New York: Macmillan, 1980).

11. Laurie Werner, "Megabuck Celebrities in the Halls of Commerce," *Cosmopolitan*, February 1987, pp. 198–201, 274, 276.

12. Judith Williamson, *Consuming Passions: Politics & Images of Popular Culture* (New York: M. Boyars, 1985).

Woman in a Man's World

1. Carroll Smith-Rosenberg, *Disorderly Conduct: Visions of Gender in Victorian America* (New York: Alfred A. Knopf, 1985). See also Elaine Showalter, ed., *These Modern Women: Autobiographical Essays from the Twenties* (New York: Feminist Press, 1978).

2. Roland Barthes, *Mythologies*, trans. by Annette Lavey (New York: Hill & Wang, 1972 [1937]).

3. Mirra Komarovsky, "The Cultural Contradictions of Sex Roles," *American Journal of Sociology* 53, No. 3 (1946): 184–89.

4. I would recommend Paula Giddings, *When and Where I Enter: The Impact of Black Women on Race and Sex in America* (New York: William Morrow, 1984).

5. Marchand, *American Dream*.

6. Ibid., p. 96.

7. Ibid., p. 101.

8. Williamson, *Consuming Passions.*

9. The emergence of toxic shock syndrome threatened this image of security. While the tampon manufacturers denied charges of responsibility, and much insistence was placed on the fault of wearers who kept tampons inserted unreasonably long, in early 1985 two major brands were recalled.

10. Baudrillard, *La société de consommation,* pp. 196–201. See also Richard Sennett, "The Age of Self-Control," *Vogue,* April 1987, pp. 362–63, 398.

The Accursed Portion

1. Georges Bataille, "La part maudite," in *Oeuvres Completes,* vol. 7 (Paris: Gallimard, 1976). In this context Julia Kristeva's *Powers of Horror: An Essay on Abjection,* trans. Leon S. Roudiez (New York: Columbia University Press, 1982), is also of interest.

2. See Chernin, *The Obsession* and *The Hungry Self.* See also Marcia Millman, *Such a Pretty Face: Being Fat in America* (New York: W.W. Norton, 1980).

3. Susie Orbach, *Fat Is a Feminist Issue: The Anti-Diet Guide to Permanent Weight Loss* (New York: Berkley Publishing, 1979).

4. See Chernin, *The Hungry Self.*

5. Noelle Caskey, "Interpreting Anorexia Nervosa," in Susan Rubin Suleiman, ed., *The Female Body in Western Culture: Contemporary Perspectives* (Cambridge: Harvard University Press), p. 187.

6. Elaine Partnow, ed., *The Quotable Woman* (New York: Anchor Books, 1978), p. 142.

7. Anne Scott Beller, *Fat and Thin: A Natural History of Obesity* (New York: Harper & Row, 1977), p. 90.

8. Jane E. Brody, "Research Lifts Blame from Many of the Obese," *New York Times,* March 27, 1987, p. C1. See also

Brody, "For Women Who Haven't Gotten The Message Yet: Thin Isn't Necessarily In," *New York Times,* March 18, 1987, p. C4.

9. Henry Fairlie, *The Seven Deadly Sins Today* (Notre Dame: University of Notre Dame Press, 1979), p. 155.
10. Chernin, *The Hungry Self,* p. 204.

Beauty Rituals

1. Marchand, *American Dream,* pp. 276–82.
2. Partnow, *Quotable Woman,* p. 410.
3. Quoted in ibid., p. 386.
4. See Victor Turner, *The Ritual Process: Structure and Anti-Structure* (Chicago: Aldine, 1969).
5. Wolfgang Lederer, *The Fear of Women* (New York: Harcourt Brace Jovanovich, 1968), p. 27.
6. Mary Douglas, *Purity and Danger: An Analysis of Concepts of Pollution and Taboo* (Boston: Ark, 1984), p. 3.
7. Kupfermann, *The MsTaken Body,* p. 57.
8. Douglas, *Purity and Danger,* p. 141.
9. Williamson, *Consuming Passions,* p. 50.
10. Anita Loos, quoted in Partnow, *Quotable Woman,* p. 43.
11. See the discussion of this point in Mona Ozouf, *La fête révolutionnaire, 1789–1799* (Paris: Gallimard, 1976).

A Gentleman and a Consumer

1. Katz and Katz, *Magazines,* pp. 703–5.
2. Ibid.
3. John Gagnon, "Physical Strength: Once of Significance," in Joseph H. Pleck and Jack Sawyer, eds., *Men and Masculinity* (Englewood Cliffs, N.J.: Prentice-Hall, 1974), pp. 139–49.
4. Baudrillard, *La société de consommation,* pp. 144–47.

5. Ibid.

6. Ibid.

7. Todd Gitlin, "We Build Excitement," in Todd Gitlin, ed., *Watching Television* (New York: Pantheon, 1986), pp. 139–40.

8. Ibid.

9. C. Wright Mills, *The Power Elite* (New York: Oxford University Press, 1956), p. 141.

10. See Diane Barthel, "A Gentleman and a Consumer: A Sociological Look at Man at His Best," paper presented at the annual meeting of the Eastern Sociological Society, March 1983, Baltimore.

11. Barbara Ehrenreich, *The Hearts of Men: American Dreams and the Flight from Commitment* (New York: Anchor Books, 1983).

Conclusion

1. Stephen Fox, *The Mirror Makers: A History of American Advertising and Its Creators* (New York: William Morrow, 1984), p. 330.

2. Anthropologist William O'Barr warns of the impact advertising may be having on children. "Television is perhaps the most important teaching medium in our society. Upon graduation from high school, the average American child has spent more time watching television than he or she has spent in classrooms, and much of this viewing has included repeated exposure to the more than 50,000 commercials produced each year. Advertising teaches a reasoning process that is different from traditional logical reasoning in that conclusions are based on limited evidence. . . . What I'm concerned about in the long run is what happens to a generation of children who are taught to draw conclusions on that kind of bias." In Bloch, "The Business of Friendly Persuasion," p. 16.

3. Schudson, *Uneasy Persuasion*, pp. 209–33.

4. Simmel, *Philosophy of Money*, p. 39.
5. Erik H. Erikson, *Childhood and Society* (New York: W. W. Norton, 1963), pp. 261–69.
6. Philip Hanson, *Advertising & Socialism: The Nature and Extent of Consumer Advertising in the Soviet Union, Poland, Hungary and Yugoslavia* (White Plains, N.Y.: International Arts and Sciences Press, 1974), pp. 153–54.
7. Baudrillard, *La société de la consommation*, p. 34.
8. Ibid., pp. 296–97.
9. As I write, Allan Bloom's *The Closing of the American Mind* is tied for first place on the *New York Times* bestseller list, which I take to be indicative of interest in contemporary American culture in general, the cultural content of the educational system in particular. See *The Closing of the American Mind: How Higher Education Has Failed Democracy and Impoverished the Souls of Today's Students* (New York: Simon & Schuster, 1987). See also E. D. Hirsch, Jr., *Cultural Literacy: What Every American Needs to Know* (Boston: Houghton Mifflin, 1987).
10. See Jürgen Habermas, "Modernity—An Incomplete Project," in Hal Foster, ed., *Postmodern Culture* (London: Pluto Press, 1985), pp. 3–15.
11. Janet Radcliffe-Richards, *The Sceptical Feminist* (London: Routledge & Kegan Paul, 1980), p. 185.

Index